Advance Praise for The 24-Hour Customer

"To many consumers, time is more important than money. Today's managers need to factor this key concept into their marketing programs. Adrian Ott provides the battle plan for doing so."

—Al and Laura Ries, bestselling authors of
The Fall of Advertising and the Rise of PR

"This outstanding book is much more than just another guide to coping with a changing world. Adrian Ott demonstrates, through solid research and compelling case histories, how customer attention has become a more precious commodity. Ott understands the way our notion of time is evolving and she explores the implications of this profound shift for gaining competitive advantage."

—Michael J. Gelb, author of *How to Think Like
Leonardo Da Vinci and Innovate Like Edison*

"In her new book, Adrian Ott has hit the nail on the head in identifying the single most important and perplexing issue facing marketers today: how to effectively deal with the time-starved, always-connected consumer. Ott asks us to consider not only alternative products or services but alternative uses of time, and this brilliant insight is a conceptual home run. This should be must-reading for any manager who wishes to acquire and retain customers in this new era."

—Peter Sealey, PhD, former CMO of
The Coca-Cola Company, adjunct professor of marketing
at the Peter F. Drucker School of Management

"*The 24-Hour Customer* contains a BIG idea that can pay off in BIG results. Adrian Ott clearly demonstrates how today's multiscreen, multitasking culture is driving vast changes in customer behavior. Leaders who want to successfully compete in today's marketplace must read this book—and act."

—Robert H. Miles, PhD, former Harvard Business School
professor; coauthor of *BIG Ideas to BIG Results*;
president, Corporate Transformation Resources

"Adrian's book outlines an innovative approach using a new lens to view the critical and increasing importance a customer's 'time' plays in their purchasing cycle. She uses this same lens to provide useful insights on how to design business strategies to create new market opportunities and achieve sustainable market position."

—Steve Steinhilber, vice president, Emerging Solutions
Ecosystems, Cisco Systems; author *Strategic Alliances*

"*The 24-Hour Customer* is a great read for any executive who needs to apply fresh thinking to products and solutions. Adrian's strategic perspective provides many 'lightbulb' moments, and, by reading this fascinating book, you'll come away with great new ideas to breathe more life and creativity into your marketing."

—Marlene Williamson, vice president, customer marketing,
Ericsson, IP and Broadband Division

"It is rare that a book introduces a new concept that is scrumptious to strategy-oriented executives' appetites, but Adrian Ott's insightful 'Money Value of Time' makes you say, 'Of course! Why didn't I think of that!' *The 24-Hour Customer* is a thoroughly enjoyable and useful book."

—Carol Mills, board member of Adobe Systems, Tekelec, and
Blue Coat Systems; former CEO of Acta Technology

"In this book, Adrian Ott appealingly explains the role of the increasingly important trade-off between time and value in driving strategy. If you understand the rules within, they will enable you to use time as a competitive advantage in vying for the attention, and wallet, of your customer."

—Saul J. Berman, vice president and global strategy and
change consulting leader, IBM Global Business Services

"Time is precious; that is why we built an entire company around helping people to be on time, or to save time getting from A to B. In *The*

24-Hour Customer, Adrian takes the concept of time in a new direction by applying it as a strategic lever—one that can influence the design, positioning, marketing, selling, and usage of your products and services in order to optimize your revenue streams. It is well worth your time to read it!"

—Peter van der Fluit, senior vice president
licensing, TomTom N.V.

"If you are as time-starved as the rest of us you must read *The 24-Hour Customer*. Adrian Ott gives the reader a crystal clear perspective on how to focus on the right strategies to break through in a world where fighting for attention is the key to winning."

—Glenn Osaka, senior vice president, Juniper Networks

"Adrian Ott lays out a compelling argument for honoring consumer's limited time and attention, especially in health care. Viewing consumer's needs through the lens of their situation, not just their wants and needs, provides a fresh perspective for marketing professionals."

—Anna Lisa Silvestre, vice president,
online services, Kaiser Permanente

"In *The 24-Hour Customer*, Adrian Ott offers a very new way of looking at things, which is both groundbreaking and pragmatic. She brilliantly observes that rather than looking only at market and product adjacencies, we should focus on time adjacencies—that is, engaging customers at those times when they are ready to take action and buy. A must-read for executives who want to succeed in today's fast-changing marketplace."

—Amanda Setili, chair and past president,
Harvard Business School Club of Atlanta;
adjunct professor, Goizueta Business School, Emory University

"*The 24-Hour Customer* by Adrian Ott is a timely and fascinating exploration of the 'fast-paced electronic' times we live in. Resting on solid market research and clearly demonstrating how deeply our 'connected' society is affected by this new economy, this book is essential reading for any company that wishes to understand the future of the marketing, social interaction, and ultimately customer satisfaction and loyalty."

—Ingrid Summerfield, president & COO,
Joie de Vivre Hospitality

"*The 24-Hour Customer* puts into magnificent perspective the increasing role of time or, better, the lack of it, in purchasing and use decisions, and Adrian Ott brilliantly succeeds in providing a very unique and useful framework to analyze, understand, and put to work the time-related trade-offs we make. For executives in small and large companies alike, this book is not to be missed."

—Robert van Eijk, vice president, Royal Philips Electronics

THE 24-HOUR
CUSTOMER

HARPER
BUSINESS

An Imprint of HarperCollins*Publishers*
www.harpercollins.com

New Rules for Winning

In a Time-Starved,

Always-Connected

Economy

11:59

7623 9380

THE 24-HOUR
CUSTOMER

ADRIAN C. OTT

For Len, Kevin, and Nicole

HarperCollins books may be purchased for educational, business, or sales promotional use. For information, please write: Special Markets Department, HarperCollins Publishers, 10 East 53rd Street, New York, NY 10022.

FIRST EDITION

Company product names and methodologies mentioned herein are the trademarks or registered trademarks of their respective owners.

Time-ographics® and Exponential Edge® are registered trademarks filed with the U.S. Patent and Trademark Office.

Designed by Kathryn Parise

Library of Congress Cataloging-in-Publication Data has been applied for.

ISBN: 978-0-06-179861-0

10 11 12 13 14 OV/RRD 10 9 8 7 6 5 4 3 2 1

CONTENTS

FOREWORD

Everyone on the Internet says they are worried about security. From financial information to family photos, our most precious information is stored on our computers. Cybercrime and identify theft are certainly things to worry about. The digital black market is thriving. A cybercrime is committed every quarter of a second, every day of the year. In fact, one of every five online shoppers in the United States will be a victim of a cybercrime. Worrying statistics all.

On the other hand, a major factor in consumer decisions on Internet security software is what program was preloaded onto their computer or what advice they were offered by salespeople or other customers in the store.

What explains this phenomenon of customers expressing a great deal of concern but not necessarily taking the time to evaluate products that will alleviate those concerns? I think Adrian's on to it: time.

There was a day when consumers' primary concerns about security software were technical product features (such as how many virus patterns were in our database and how many different types of files we could scan). Today, the primary concern is time: Who is going to allow me to stop worrying about Internet security the fastest? Who is going to get me protected without slowing my computer down?

Now this requires a great deal of trust. If customers didn't trust that Symantec was going to keep up with technology developments and new threats, then it wouldn't matter if our software was preloaded on every computer or the fastest on the planet. They wouldn't buy it at any price, even free—and free is a real option for plain-vanilla antivirus software.

Customers want to "set it and forget it" when it comes to security software, and forgetting it requires both that they believe they are protected and that the software doesn't intrude on their attention.

When customers do start paying attention to security software, it's usually associated with one of two events—they're purchasing a new computer or they, a friend, or a relative has been a victim of malware, identity theft, or another cybercrime. These unfortunate, and sometimes very costly, incidents focus their attention on security software, but only momentarily—they seek out a security solution that can allow them to go back to not worrying about Internet security as soon as possible.

At Symantec, we've learned that to be successful we need to understand the cycles of customer attention and the triggers that cause customers to pay more attention, but also how we can appropriately allow them to feel at ease and redirect their attention to other things.

I've known Adrian Ott for more than 20 years—first when we worked together at Hewlett Packard (HP), and then as her firm has done a series of projects for me since I came to Symantec. Over that time I've watched her consistently see not only what's ahead, but what's around the corner or lurking in the alley. Adrian has always had a unique ability to see how several different trends are coming together to form something completely new. But more important, she's been able to help me see how to take advantage of the opportunities presented by the convergence of trends.

A good example is Adrian's work on the Garage Program while we worked together at HP. We created the Garage Program to help HP build bridges to the startup community in Silicon Valley and beyond. Although HP is in many ways the original Silicon Valley startup, it was an island at that time. There was a lot of innovation happening at HP, but even more happening all around us, which we weren't connected to. Adrian and her team built a program that served a dual purpose: packaging HP products in ways that would be useful to startups and help them grow their businesses, and building bridges to the entrepreneurial ecosystem, such as the venture capitalists, academic community, government entities, and incubators, to identify promising technologies that might be of interest to future HP product development efforts.

Adrian was able to build partnerships inside and outside of HP—including with Microsoft and several national governments, as well as the more obvious connections with venture capitalists and academics. As a result of her leadership, the Garage Program business grew to $250 million in annual revenue in a short period of time. She was recognized in HP's 2000 annual report for "infusing HP with new revenue streams and technology and business models."

I sincerely believe that in this book, Adrian has identified another one of these key moments when several trends converge to create something very different. We've all felt the growing pressure of time constraints over the last two decades. Every minute we gain from productivity tools, and being able to "work anywhere," seems to be canceled out by two minutes of additional demands on our time.

But very few companies seem to have responded systematically to the increasing time pressures and distractions that we all face. While there are lots of new channels and "innovative" marketing programs, they in the end come back to the same messages about product functionality. They aren't taking into account the impact of time and attention. Social media, for instance, is a new approach to marketing but if you're using the same old messages, you're not likely to experience much success. There's no question that there are new rules—but figuring out what those rules are while you're running full speed, dealing with changing technology and evolving competitors and short on time, is difficult.

Later in the book you'll read about one of Symantec's recent successes with the new rules: an effort to capture the time and attention of chief information officers (CIOs). Symantec's suite of corporate security and compliance tools are ranked very highly, but we had trouble getting CIO attention to focus on a company that they had wrongly equated only with antivirus software. We had to find a way to break through these CIOs' time barriers so we could tell our story. We knew that if we could capture just a little time and attention, our products would be appealing and could solve the highest-priority problems of CIOs and their companies. By creating a benchmark on security and compliance, we were able to do just that. Our success with CIOs was due to understanding that our problem wasn't price or product features, it was customer time and attention. To break through the CIOs' time barriers, we had to do something to convince them that they should shift their attention and spend some time with us. "Shouting" louder to try to get their attention—whether that was via a very expensive advertising campaign or by cutting prices dramatically—wouldn't have worked, and it would have done damage to our bottom line.

Time and attention are equally important in the consumer market. Just one of the ways that this has affected Symantec is our realization of the role time—or put another way, speed—affects our customers. Over the years we've noticed a steady shift in customer priorities from safety to speed. This is not to imply that customers didn't care about speed in the past, just that speed has become a much bigger issue—this despite the fact that threats have grown exponentially. In 2009 alone, we expected roughly 2.5 million new threats to emerge. But while threats have increased, customers have become less willing to tolerate any security product that slows down their computers or their Web-browsing, no matter how secure it keeps them. A security product that noticeably slows performance will be turned off by many users, leaving them wholly unprotected. So we had to fundamentally rethink the engineering of our products to ensure they delivered security without costing the customer time. I'll bet you won't be surprised to hear that as our products have gotten faster, our customer satisfaction has rapidly increased. Another way we've tried to address customers' security worries while solving their time problem is with an integrated backup and security product called Norton 360. Customers who use both security and backup have significantly higher retention rates than those who use just one of the products. I strongly believe that the reason for our success with Norton 360 can be traced to time and attention. We were able to make the formerly complicated functions simple, and thereby save customers a great deal of time and allow them to focus their attention elsewhere.

In the consumer space we've succeeded by saving customers time and attention. But it's never just a question of saving time and deflecting attention. We've found that customers won't renew their products if we are "quiet" all the time. The customer doesn't perceive value from a product that is too "set it and forget it"—they have no idea what the security product is doing for them. You can't work so hard to save customers' time and attention that they decide come renewal time that you don't add any value. As you can see, profiting from the economics of time and attention requires some careful thought and planning.

This is just one of the ways that thinking about your customers' time and attention will require you to consider much more than product features and price. In a world where time constraints dominate, your competition is very different. It's not just companies that make similar products—it's every product or activity that the customer may be spending time and attention on. At the same time, as Adrian shows, there are terrific opportunities for growth that come from thinking not just about adjacent product markets but about adjacent and overlapping time markets.

Throughout the years I've known Adrian, I've come to trust her instincts and her insights. When she shared her thinking with me about how time and attention were changing the rules, the gears in my mind started turning right away. Stepping back and looking at our big wins and our less successful initiatives over the last few years, I immediately saw how Adrian's approach helped explain what had worked and what hadn't. Over the last few months as I've thought further about Adrian's framework, I've seen even more applications.

That's why I highly recommend this book. The new rules are already governing how your customers are making decisions. The only question is whether you will start playing by the new rules and winning customer attention or will let time pass you by.

—*Janice Chaffin, President, Symantec Consumer Group*

INTRODUCTION

■

So Many Products, So Little Time

We're all familiar with paying extra because we've run out of time. How often have you purchased something at a significant markup at the airport—say a headset for your cell phone—because you misplaced or forgot yours and didn't have time to retrieve it? How many times have you paid the premium for overnight delivery because you ran late on a deadline? Paying for convenience, then, isn't a new phenomenon, per se. But the tradeoffs we make between time and value are increasingly escaping the airport concession and hotel gift shop. Companies that understand the value of time and, in doing so, build their products or services around the customer's willingness to invest precious time and attention are gaining competitive traction in markets where their competitors are increasingly slipping. Such companies are also capturing new product and service opportunities in previously undefined market categories.

Consider Voice2insight, a service that capitalizes on a time-centric mind-set. Voice2insight's mobile solution allows busy professionals to capture the knowledge and action items from meetings and helps to move these processes forward. The company came to its solution after observing a common challenge: like most busy executives, you have probably experienced days when you were rushing from meeting to meeting struggling to keep up with voicemail and email. No doubt you've more than once come to the end of a busy day and realized that you agreed to do something—but you just can't remember what it was and can't find a reference to it in your notes. In all the scurrying and scrambling, some of your "to-do's" get lost. This problem is not unique to executives; salespeople experience it as well. In the rush to get from one sales call to another, important action items get lost and a golden sales opportunity falls through. Days are so full it's no wonder that something slips through the cracks: there's simply no time.

The Voice2insight service allows sales personnel and busy executives to pick up their cell phones as they are leaving a meeting and create a detailed voice record of the knowledge gained during the meeting and the next steps to take. The automated voice response system prompts the caller for specific information, and the service transcribes the answers and inputs the responses into the appropriate back-office systems. The user is then free to focus on his or her next meeting.

Meanwhile, the Voice2insight system updates Customer Relationship Management (CRM) records. Action items are assigned; meetings are scheduled; and email thank-you's are sent. The salesperson is relieved of a time-consuming administrative burden, creating more time to sell. This is not just theoretical: according to Matt Tippetts, CEO of Voice2insight, one Fortune 500 company found that the Voice2insight solution would generate an additional 5 percent in revenue per representative by enabling more customer calls per week.[1]

Salespeople, just like the rest of us, are factoring time relative to product value more frequently into their decision-making. One of the first times I became really aware of how I evaluate time relative to value was about five years ago, when I received an early-model MP3 player. I thought it would be helpful to listen to music or audio books while running.

Now, I'm not exactly a tech geek, but I have worked in, around, and with technology companies for most of my 20-plus-year career. Tech gadgets don't intimidate me. In many ways, I am an early adopter. My home office is littered with technology prototypes from my firm's work to shape new product concepts and go-to-market strategies for clients. In addition, my husband is a chief technology officer for a mobile tech company and has contributed to several technology standards. Consequently, I often find myself acting as a guinea pig for the latest technology concoction or beta software release.

Still, my MP3 player sat gathering dust. I never got around to loading any music on it, much less actually using it. Then I received an iPod as a gift, and it has been a constant companion ever since. I love my iPod so much, I purchased more for members of my family.

This story may seem like fairly typical consumer purchase and use decisions—the kind of decision, but for the product name, that would easily have fit the Awareness, Consideration, Preference, and Purchase models taught in marketing classes since the 1950s. But the story, like Voice2insight, actually turns on a new dynamic that has been growing steadily more important for the last 20 years—one that many companies and marketing executives still fail to consider: time.

Today, time isn't money. Time is more important than money. It's certainly more important than brand recognition, product features, authenticity, or most of the other factors that usually figure into an executive's product plans. Time isn't the only consideration for customers, but it is the most consistently overlooked and misunderstood factor driving customer decisions.

How Time and Attention Drive Customer Decision-Making

When you buy yet another cell phone headset in the airport, you're making a decision based on time. You're usually not really considering product alternatives. You're not comparing this headset to that headset, or calculating your preference for listening to the music loaded on your phone versus the music on your computer versus the music on the plane's audio system. You're weighing time versus cost: the productive time you'll lose by not being able to make calls in the car, plus the time to find, drive to, and purchase a headset at your destination, plus the time to think about the decision while in the airport.

My adoption of the iPod and not the MP3 player wasn't driven by sleek design or hip advertising; it was driven by confidence that I wouldn't have to spend time making the thing work. I knew going in that music I bought from iTunes would play on the iPod and that the device would sync and charge as soon as I connected it to my PC. I wouldn't have to waste any time fiddling with settings, dragging and dropping files, wondering about file format compatibility, etc., etc. Most of all, the brand promise from Apple said to me, "It just works. No *time* required."

Of course, all time is not created equal. There are many things customers want to spend time on as well as the many they don't. The importance of time is captured in the old adage about land: "They aren't making any more of it." In fact, for me and probably for you and your customers, it actually seems like less is being made of it every day.

The most valuable time for everyone—consumers, executives, and marketers—is time where attention is focused. And there truly is less of that for almost everyone. Consider that every aspect of your business impacts your customers' time and attention—from product design decisions to marketing programs to channels of distribution to customer service. Product and service decisions made with time- and attention-based mindsets can move customers decisively in your favor rather than negatively against it. Companies that learn how to use limited time and attention to their advantage will gain a huge edge over their competition. That's what this book is about.

A Fraction of Time Is Spent Buying

I frequently hear executives lament, "The market has become so competitive. Every day new players appear that eat into our margins and kill our sales!" It's true that customer choices in virtually every product category have dramatically increased over the last 30 years, a trend driven by a variety of factors, such as deregulation, globalization, and the Internet. But the real issue is not increased competition. It's the collision of those increased choices with the immovable barrier of time.

Americans have a reputation for shopping. Consumers drive the national economy, yet most Americans actually devote relatively little time to making purchases. Despite popular stereotypes of "shopaholics" and "mall rats," only 42 percent of Americans report that they enjoy buying goods and services. Forty-eight percent describe it as "just something they have to do."[2]

These preferences show up in the amount of time Americans devote to shopping. The U.S. Bureau of Labor Statistics reports that Americans spend about 28 minutes per day purchasing goods and services—between 2 and 3 percent of waking hours.[3] Compared to what they spend on leisure activities and household chores such as cleaning and cooking, those 28 minutes Americans spend shopping are but a fraction.[4] Although the data are more sporadic, our research suggests that this situation is the same in other industrialized countries as well. Figure I-1 highlights this comparison.

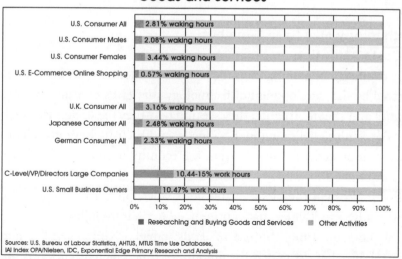

Percentage of Time Used to Research and Buy Goods and Services

Sources: U.S. Bureau of Labour Statistics, AHTUS, MTUS Time Use Databases, IAI Index OPA/Nielsen, IDC, Exponential Edge Primary Research and Analysis

Figure I–1: Customers devote a small fraction of their time to researching, evaluating, and purchasing products and services.[5]

Consumers are not spending the entire 28 minutes actually buying, either. That half-hour includes other elements of the buying cycle, such as browsing offerings in a store or researching items online.[6]

The situation is similar in the business-to-business sector. Research conducted by my firm, and others, found that business executives (outside of the procurement function) spend a small fraction of their time (10 to 15 percent) evaluating noncommodity purchases.[7] During this time executives are researching via media and Internet sources, speaking with colleagues about solutions and references, reading vendor collateral and websites, evaluating options, speaking with the vendor, and approving purchase orders.[8]

We are in an era of too many choices competing for too little time. The proliferation of products from around the globe has resulted in a plethora of options for buyers. As a result, the concept of traditional customer loyalty has suffered continuous decline from the time when our grandparents "always bought Fords." A study by the CMO Council and Pointer Media Network further reveals that 80 percent of loyal brand sales are attributed to only 2.5 percent of shoppers, not 80/20 as previously thought.[9] We need to find a better way.

Technology May Save Time but It Costs Attention

The challenge of gaining customer time and attention has been exacerbated by the development of technology that gives consumers more control over the information they see and how they see it. Services such as TiVo, Hulu, satellite radio, RSS feeds, and their ilk have given consumers unprecedented liberty from the tyranny of mass media. They no longer need to watch broadcast television (or the ads that go along with it). Nor will they look at the newspaper, preferring a stream of news via RSS or Twitter that's customized to their interests.

At the same time, the use of iPods, tablets, Nintendo DSs, and smartphones has decreased the amount of time when attention is not diluted by some form of media (be it music or a phone call). It's not just teenagers that are texting while watching TV, or talking on the cell phone at the dinner table. No doubt, our society is connected and addicted.

The constant use of media, including social media, led Pope Benedict XVI to proclaim (via the Vatican's YouTube channel, of course) that social networking sites such as Facebook and MySpace should be praised for forging friendships and understanding, but cautioned that online networking could isolate people from real social interaction. In response, many Roman Catholic bishops in Italy urged their parishioners to stop using social networking or text messaging for Lent in 2009.[10] In the tradition of giving up something of value such as chocolate, cigarettes, or red meat for this 40-day holy period, the no-technology fast was viewed as a commensurately difficult sacrifice.

When your target customer is watching a movie on his iPad or negotiating a contract on her smartphone, it doesn't matter how attractive your spokesperson is, how clever your ad is, or how compelling your product is. Your message is simply not going to get through.

There Are No Winners in the Attention Arms Race

The flood of products claiming some portion of customers' time has driven a war for attention, mostly to the benefit of the companies that sell advertising space. Consider the cost of a commercial on the Super Bowl today versus 15 years ago. A few rules of thumb have emerged, and everyone has pounced: increase the volume; sex sells; animals are cute; buy one, get one free!

The Web has also seen its share of these gimmicks: get-rich-quick Tweets blasting into the Twitter-void, spam blogs (splogs), and the infamous pop-ups and flashing banners competing to win the prize for the world's most annoying ways to get attention. As a result, customers have developed highly evolved attentional filters that tune out these demands on their attention. They have become more protective of their time and are more vigilant against anything that hints of advertising, spam, telephone solicitation, and self-promotion.

We all know, even if we are afraid to admit it, that everyone loses the attention arms race. As more companies adopt the same techniques in a desperate attempt to gain an attention foothold, consumers become more sophisticated at tuning out what's thrown at them. When was the last time you remember taking notice of a banner on a Web page? Or registering what was on a billboard as you drove past?

But it's even worse than it seems. Attention isn't a zero-sum game— it's a negative-sum game, you might say, because of a factor psychologists call attentional blink. Studies have found that when participants focus attention on a specific piece of information, a strange gap appears in their ability to pay attention immediately afterward. The mind is so focused that when it moves away from that initial object, it relaxes and doesn't register anything. It is as if the brain develops a temporary blind spot.

One study that illustrated this phenomenon flashed a series of words to participants every 10 seconds. The participants were asked to search for two particular words. People are normally very good at finding the words in this test, with 80 percent accuracy.[11]

When researchers placed the two words directly after each other in close succession, however, researchers found that the correct reporting of the second word fell to zero accuracy—complete lack of recognition. Further psychological studies reveal that this phenomenon also affects hearing. It seems that attentional blink affects the brain, not just the eyes.[12]

Yet most executives and marketers continue to fight the same war for attention with the same old weapons. Product features, advertising, and public relations still hold pride of place in the marketing tool kit. But without a clear understanding of the forces of time and attention, they just don't cut it anymore. Customers are too distracted.

Competition Based on Time

When viewed in the overall context of time—24 hours per day, or 1,440 minutes—we begin to understand the tremendous competition for time that exists, not just within a particular category, but across all products and services that reach customers. A business gets only a small share of customer time, and customers quickly dismiss irrelevant offerings as "background noise." Such offerings are out of sync with the cadence and rhythm of their lives.

With a proliferation of offerings from around the world and the relatively fixed constraint of purchasing time, markets have become like a stroll down Times Square in New York—flashing lights, blasting car horns, and people begging for attention. To cope with overstimulation, customers ultimately determine what will fit in their timeframe. The customer time barrier has a profound effect on how the competitive landscape is shaped.

Michael Porter, in his classic book *Competitive Strategy*, identifies substitutes in an industry as a critical element in the five forces of competition model. An analysis of substitutes would suggest that in addition to comparing competing restaurants, the substitute of dinner at home (through the act of buying groceries) should be considered in the competitive analysis. They all serve the function of eating a meal.

In *Blue Ocean Strategy*, W. Chan Kim and Renée Maubourgne built upon this approach with the concept of alternatives. Alternatives present themselves when we look beyond an industry boundary (restaurants/meals) to take a cross-industry look at where alternatives could be purchased. For example, couples looking for a night out aren't just choosing between restaurants; they are choosing between a meal and a movie. The theater is as much a competitor to the restaurant as are other restaurants.

Both substitutes and alternatives are commerce related. Choosing among options involves comparing relative attributes and benefits. Certainly, these comparisons are important.

In this book I am sharing a new dimension that should be considered to address our media-rich, mobile, multitasking world. We are faced not just with alternative product offerings but alternative uses of time—some of which are not commerce related. When we have a spare moment, do we use it to buy new pet supplies online, play with our children, log in to a social network to see what's new with our friends, search for research to support a project at work, or check out that new YouTube video a colleague just sent in an email? Or all of the above?

To break the time barrier, we need to look beyond product alternatives, whether in a given industry or across industries. Instead, to truly understand the competitive landscape we need to identify alternative uses of time, such as social networks, family, chores, email, and digital devices that may pull a customer in a particular direction.

With a time and attention landscape defined, we can devise ways to earn a share of customer time that enables product and service adoption. Throughout the book, I'll explore the concept of customer time and attention and identify factors that compel customers to spend time with some offerings but not others.

Time as Competitive Advantage

If you doubt the power of time to create and sustain competitive advantage, consider the recent challenges faced by Ty's Beanie Babies. Back in the late 1990s, a good friend shared with me tales of searching out the newest "gotta have it" Beanie Baby for his daughter. He wasn't alone. Beanie Babies, small stuffed animals sold through specialty retailers, were the rage among school-age children and collectors. As new animals were introduced, shortages occurred and an entire aftermarket economy emerged for reselling the toys at a markup. Some Beanie Babies that normally retailed from $5 to $10 were selling for as much as $5,000 for particularly hard-to-find models.

Ten years later, my daughter was the same age as my friend's was then, and she was hooked on adorable plush animals too—but not Beanie Babies. Webkinz were my daughter's vice. Webkinz are like Beanie Babies, but with an Internet component. Webkinz World is a virtual online playground that mirrors the offline world with an avatar of your child's toy. Children can chat, purchase accessories, and decorate their virtual worlds. Ganz, the makers of Webkinz, had an audience of 6 million and more than $100 million in retail sales in 2008. [13]

Ty tried to recapture success with its Beanie Babies 2.0 virtual world. By traditional marketing standards, Ty appeared to be doing everything right. They had a brand name that is recognized worldwide (a marketer's holy grail), a lower price point, and alternative distribution channels.[14]

But it was too late. The issue was not features or price or brand recognition; the issue was time. Most parents limit how long their children can spend online. Webkinz had a hammerlock on that time, with users spending an average of 154 minutes on the Webkinz site each month.[15] A child can't move her customized room from Webkinz World to the Beanie Babies World, and can't add on the time to build up a similar customized room in Beanie Babies. As of January 2010, Webkinz.com realized more than 4.5 million unique visitors versus under 300,000 unique visitors for Ty.com—more than 16 times the traffic.[16]

The main point of the story is that traditional customer analysis, at least insofar as it excludes time, is far less useful than it used to be. Countless dollars are spent on understanding customer preference, brand recognition, and product satisfaction; virtually none is spent on customer time. Ask your friends and colleagues and it won't take long to hear war stories about how the businesses they interact with waste their time. But this goes far beyond call centers, customer experience, and usability. There are vast white-space opportunities to be captured because so few businesses use this to their advantage.

Innovators and marketers need more than the usual brand equity and satisfaction scores. They need a systematic framework for evaluating and acting upon time and attention constraints. As we saw with the iPod and Voice2insight examples, the time and attention required to evaluate, set up, and consume an offering relative to the expected value can spell the difference between success and failure. We will explore how customers prioritize and make such tradeoffs between time and value.

Customer Time-Value and the Time-ographics Framework

So how should one think about customer time to gain competitive advantage? What is needed is a time- and attention-centered worldview, what I call a Customer Time-Value mindset. One way to approach this is through a Time-ographics[17] analysis, which provides a lens for businesses to determine customer time and attention priorities for their offering. We all make time and attention allocation decisions every day. Similarly, we prioritize the goods and services that we buy according to whether we would like to spend time or minimize time and attention devoted to it (consider how much time and attention you devote to selecting socks relative to a critical business decision). Ultimately, a product or service is prioritized by the customer into one of four quadrant categories based on the context and constraints. The four quadrant categories are: motivation, habit, convenience, and value. In chapter 1, I will share this four-quadrant framework in more detail.

A Customer Time-Value mindset helps to answer questions such as:

1. How do I gain sustainable market traction in a distracted world?
2. How do I utilize a Customer Time-Value approach to innovate new opportunities?
3. How do I ensure customer adoption for my new offering?
4. How can I avoid customer defection due to actions by my competitors?

The Approach

This work is the culmination of three-and-a-half years of research and a 20-plus-year career in strategy, marketing, and high technology. I have drawn upon a variety of sources and experiences to develop the concepts in this book, including work with Fortune 500 companies and venture-backed startups, interviews, discussions with more than 200 industry executives, and reviews of the latest academic research, particularly in the areas of attention, multitasking, habit development, the Internet, and customer behavior.

Through my research and client work, I have connected the dots from disparate disciplines and sources, including mobile technology, psychology, brain physiology, marketing, behavioral economics, time-use statistics, Internet, social media, and consulting, into a digestible approach to gaining traction with today's busy customer.

My approach and mindset is that of a business executive. Having devoted the bulk of my career leading, defining, and executing real-world product and service strategies at such market-leading companies as HP, AT&T (formerly Pacific Bell), and Clorox, I've experienced firsthand what works and doesn't work. Like you, I know what it is like to lie awake at night thinking about what is needed for a new offering to succeed in the market. Each experience provided a rich set of real-world lessons.

This book highlights companies that have applied a customer time- and attention-centric lens to their business. Because this is based on best practices in an emerging discipline (a.k.a. "next practices"), no single company has executed all of the exercises or processes that I will demonstrate here. Similarly, the company case studies that I highlight may not have used my terms to describe their approach (or used any names at all, for that matter), but they are applying a Customer Time-Value mindset and many of the new rules that became apparent to me as I looked across companies for commonalities.[18] As you know, businesses and customers are complex, and they have a network of diverse driving factors; it would be misleading to tell you that any framework or approach works in every situation. What I hope to provide is a method you can use to determine which elements apply best to your situation and a tool kit from which you can choose the most appropriate strategies in this emerging discipline.

What's in the Book?

The chapters that follow explore how to apply a Customer Time-Value mindset to your business using case studies from companies such as Johnson & Johnson, Zipcar, Nike, Cisco, Google, P&G, Amazon, and many innovative start-ups.

Chapters 1 and 2 trace the history of increasing customer distraction and explain what is really happening in the minds of distracted and multitasking customers. I'll explain the Time-ographics four-quadrant framework in detail and show how some companies are using an understanding of customer time and attention to gain traction and hold off competitors. I will also share an overview of key strategies and tools that are available to executives. These management tools will be demonstrated in the chapters that follow.

Chapters 3 through 6 delve deeper into the quadrants described in the framework and explain strategies for gaining and holding a position in the various quadrants. I'll discuss how customer habits, motivations, and convenience affect customer decisions and time priorities.

Chapters 7 and 8 address how to apply a Customer Time-Value mindset within your innovation and marketing plans. I'll also take a look at where technology is taking us in terms of time and attention, and how to continue to gain and maintain traction as markets change.

I recognize that, just like your customers, you're constantly bombarded by interruptions and demands on your time and attention. To make the reading easier, a summary in the form of a "Two-Minute Takeaway" is available at the end of each chapter to enable you to skim the key points and return later to refresh your memory quickly when the time is right.

I will use the term "products" to represent "products," "services," or "programs." The concepts in this book apply to all of these offerings. Whether you are charged with innovating products and services to consumers or business customers, I hope you gain many interesting ideas and practices to apply to your company in the pages that follow.[19]

1

THE MONEY VALUE OF TIME

"The decline in the cost of IT hardware has been so rapid that it's tempting to assume it explains all the changes that take place in economy and society. But in our lifetime, we've witnessed a second price change that's as jolting as the one in hardware; the cost of time has increased . . . human time is used in every productive process and every consumption activity, so changes in the cost of time have pervasive effects on the economy and society."[1]
Dr. Paul Romer, developer of New Growth Theory,
Senior Fellow, Stanford University Center
for Economic Policy Research

While fishing for a new product idea a few years ago, some tech types at Nike noticed something about the runners they saw near the company's Beaverton, Oregon, campus: they were all wearing ear buds and listening to music during their workouts.[2] After further investigation, they learned that 50 percent of iPod users exercised while listening to the music players.[3]

Nike and Apple responded to this opportunity with the Nike+ Sport Kit, a tool that lets runners know how far and how fast they have run. The kit contains a wireless sensor that tucks into the sole of the Nike shoe and a corresponding receiver that plugs into an iPod. As the athlete runs, the sensor measures the runner's pace and sends information to the iPod, where it gets synced up with the runner's time to calculate distance, pace, calories burned, and other relevant details.

Other exercise-measurement products existed during that time, but they did not carry the guaranteed usability that is synonymous with the iPod. They also did not offer the increased benefit of a website for easy data comparison. At the end of a workout, runners plug their iPod into a PC, and their workout data will upload to the Nike+ website. There, they can track their time and distance compared with previous runs, evaluate their mile splits, and even sign up to "race" another Nike+ user anywhere in the world. They can also find workout and diet suggestions and buy more Nike products.

No doubt, this is an impressive product and the application of wireless technology in the shoe is innovative. But that's not the important part of the Nike+ story. The real win comes from the fact that Nike changed the nature of their customer interactions from a periodic, transactional shoe purchase to a consistent integrated relationship with the runner. Nike figured out how to use time to differentiate its products and provide extra value to customers. Remarkably, it's value that increases with every use, making it harder for competitors to catch the attention of Nike's customers. As of this writing, more than 210 million miles have been logged by users on the Nike+ website. That's equivalent to 8,486 laps around the world by loyal Nike customers.[4]

Nike is reaping the benefits of these efforts: its running-shoe market share has enjoyed a 13 percentage point gain since the launch of the Nike+, from 48 percent to 61 percent in 2008.[5] Nike is playing by the new rules—and winning.

Time, Attention, and the 24-Hour Customer

The success of the Nike+ has come during an era of real challenges for businesses. Consumers are spending only about 28 minutes each day researching and buying goods and services—that's less than 3 percent of waking hours.[6] In other industrialized countries, the figures appear to be similar. And despite the 24/7 availability afforded by the Internet, U.S. customers spend less than six minutes a day on e-commerce sites—that's less than 1 percent of waking hours—a small window of time relative to the thousands of e-commerce websites vying for attention.[7]

As I shared in the introduction, even business-to-business–sector executives making noncommodity purchases spend a fraction of their time doing this (between 10 and 15 percent of working hours).[8] They are not lining up to meet with vendors or to read marketing materials on top of an already overflowing in-box.

It would seem logical that increasing the available opportunities for customers to buy would have increased the amount of time customers spend buying. However, the introduction of around-the-clock e-commerce and 24-hour store schedules has not significantly changed the amount of purchase time. Despite the opportunity to shop in your slippers at midnight, the time spent on shopping and services in the United States has remained relatively steady from 2003 to 2008 even when travel to and from a store is excluded from consideration. In fact, U.S. time-use studies have shown that the amount of time spent purchasing goods and services has remained relatively constant since the 1960s (see Figure 1–1).[9] Viewed together, the increase in the number of available products coupled with the relatively static time spent buying present a considerable challenge for executives.

Ultimately, more and more goods and services are attempting to push through a small window of time. Meanwhile, the amount of information available on the Internet has exploded. It's like an assembly line where there is capacity upstream to build widgets, but everything is piling up at the warehouse because there are not enough trucks to ship the final widgets to the consumer. A bottleneck of time prevents many offerings from ever reaching their intended audience.

Although we know that the amount of time consumers spend shopping has not changed over the past four decades,[10] what *has* changed in that time is the amount of distraction that is encountered during those 28 minutes. A housewife grocery shopping in 1960 saw only products on the shelves, a daily newspaper, and a limited number of broadcast TV

Time Spent Purchasing Goods and Services Has Remained Constant While Products Have Proliferated

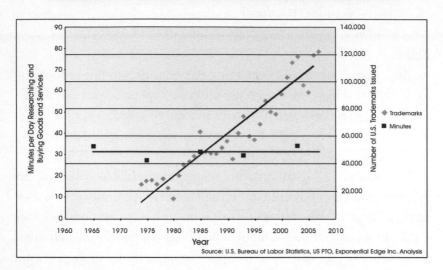

Figure 1–1: Although product choices have grown significantly, the amount of time U.S. consumers devote to shopping has remained relatively constant since the 1960s.[11]

and radio channels. Today, the devices and inputs we choose to entertain ourselves beyond radios and televisions—including smartphones, MP3 players, electronic book readers, and PCs—provide constant, self-created distraction. Couple those with the inputs we don't choose (commercial breaks, pop-ups and banner ads, taxi-top advertisements, dinner-hour telemarketers, cable TV piped into airport terminals), and it is a guarantee that we are incapable of paying undivided attention during most of our waking day. There is a time barrier *and* an attention barrier, and they work together to narrow the window of opportunity for products to take hold.

Constant Distraction Calls for New Rules

Many businesses are responding to these dynamics simply by getting louder. They develop the flashiest copy or Internet banner they can come up with and put it everywhere they can afford (and some places they can't): Super Bowl commercials, Times Square billboards, Facebook, Twitter, Google, full-page newspaper ads.

With all due respect to the advertising industry, it is not working. The target audience is savvier than ever. They no longer tolerate the messages that marketers want to send. Instead, they use the ad-skipping functionality of TiVo or other DVR devices. They subscribe to the Kindle version of the *Wall Street Journal* so they get only the content. They delete voicemails and don't return sales calls. They tune out the omnipresent Web banner ads and they don't even see the links promoted in Google's right-hand gutter—a 2009 report from comScore estimated that just 8 percent of Internet users are responsible for 85 percent of all ad clicks.[12] Businesses are stuck trying to get through to customers that are actively avoiding them, or to consumers who are so oversaturated with marketing messages in media that they can't see or hear even the content that would interest them.

There is another way. Rather than fighting against the barriers of time and attention, why not use them to build advantage? I have discovered in my research and through my work in Silicon Valley that there are certain rules or forces that compel customers to willingly spend more time on certain activities such as spending hours surfing the Web or on products such as Nike+. Conversely, there are other products that cause customers to actively shun them and say, "I have no time for this!" Understanding the differences and knowing how to work for, rather than against, these forces are essential new rules for winning in a time-starved, always-connected economy. We will explore these new rules throughout this book. They are summarized in Table 1–1.

By understanding the broader picture as to how runners multitask, Nike found a white-space opportunity between existing product categories (the running shoe and the iPod) that allowed runners to keep doing what they had been doing before—only better. Such a little thing resulted in the sale of one million Nike+ Sport Kits in their first year on the market. And users who synced their data with the Nike+ website willingly increased the amount of time they spent with Nike top of mind. Nike didn't demand time and attention. It earned them by

Then vs. Now

OLD RULES	NEW RULES
Get louder-cut through customer distraction	Capture opportunities that emerge from multitasking and distraction
Differentiate on product features	Differentiate on customer time priorities
View customers as static: e.g., psychographic preferences ("urban chic")	View customers as situational: e.g., behavioral time preferences and triggers
Grow through product adjacencies	Grow by shifting time boundaries
Focus on labor time as an input into production and price	Focus on customer time to evaluate, set up and consume
Create advantage by dominating mass media and retail distribution	Create advantage through customer inertia and time-relevant value

Table 1–1: New Rules for Winning in a Time-Starved, Always-Connected Economy

understanding the customer's propensity for spending time and by developing a product that added value within those time constraints. By automatically uploading the running data to the Nike+ website, trend and training information cannot be easily transferred to a competitor, creating incentive for the runner to return to Nike+. As a result, Nike ultimately captured time, attention, and competitive advantage.

To help companies find unique opportunities under the new rules, there are two important time-and-attention-based concepts and processes. To understand, they are:

- the Time-Value Tradeoff
- Customer Time-ographics Analysis

The Time-Value Tradeoff

Have you ever gone to the store intending to buy two items and walked out with a shopping cart full of purchases? Have you ever received an

Internet offer for something that was available for free but hesitated when it came time to register your email address? This is the Time-Value Tradeoff in action.

The Time-Value Tradeoff is the time-and-attention calculation that every customer tallies in his or her head before buying a product or signing up for a service. We purchase additional goods at the store because the time saved by stocking up today exceeds the perceived cost of a subsequent trip. Or we hesitate to register for free Internet services because we know that we will "pay" with time spent erasing spam from our in-boxes.

The Time-Value Tradeoff causes the customer to answer the question "Is it worth it?" in a way that is not just about price and features. The tradeoff occurs with nonpurchasing decisions as well. If someone invites you to a club meeting or conference, you ask yourself, "Will the value of what I learn or people that I meet be worth my time?"

A simple way to think about the Time-Value Tradeoff is through the following equation:[13]

$$Value > Price + Customer\ Time\ Investment$$

The perceived value of the product simply must exceed the price of the good *plus* the customer time investment required to use it. Although economists have always included "other factors" in value, customers weigh the cost of time more heavily today. What was a small "t" for time investment in the past (not a big consideration) is now a capital "T" (a big consideration) in the purchase equation.

We can see this effect with the proliferation of free offers. The economic laws of supply and demand would argue that a free product will generate demand.[14] Lower the price and customers will buy, right? Take the example I gave in the introduction of my first MP3 player. Even though the product was free to me (it was a gift), the time required to learn how to use it exceeded the value I anticipated receiving from it, and so it gathered dust on my shelf.

This equation factors into my evaluation of any new product regardless of whether it is free. Do you do the same? Understanding Time-

Value Tradeoffs associated with your products is one of the new rules for winning in today's economy.

Traditional economics tends to focus on the time to produce the good (i.e. labor). Under the new rules, innovators and marketers need to understand the perspective of the customers' time to evaluate, set up, and consume the good—time is viewed through the lens of purchase and consumption instead of production. These consumption-related elements help to determine whether the balance of time and value fall into or out of a favorable position for product adoption. *For innovators and marketers it is not about the TIME value of MONEY, it is about the MONEY value of TIME.*

Segmenting Customer Time and Attention Priorities

The fact that people have preferences when it comes to their time and attention should make clear that not all time is equal. This is not just the subjective observation of harried executives—it is a documented law of physics. Albert Einstein's theory of special relativity says that time passes more or less quickly depending on whether the observer himself is in motion. While the physics don't truly apply (no one on earth is moving fast enough to affect the flow of time), the implication certainly does.

A different customer who spends time in ways other than I do may have had a very different experience with that MP3 player. A die-hard music lover, for example, or a runner who can't leave the house without a personal soundtrack may have assigned a higher value to the MP3's functions, thus providing more leeway in the areas of price and time investment. These factors are very much dependent upon a person's context as it relates to the person's time and attention, known for our purposes as customer Time-ographics. Time-ographics maps a customer's time and attention in relation to an activity or product.

People measure their time differently depending on what they are doing, and willingly dedicate attention over a period of time depending on how they perceive its value. Hours spent playing with the kids or preparing for an important meeting are considered "well spent"; time spent in line at the post office is "wasted."

Time, of course, is perceived—and not very accurately. Recent studies show that when there is a sole, single-file line, people believe they spent less time waiting in it than people who passed the same amount of time in one of many grocery store lines. The likely culprit is that when there are multiple lines at the grocery store, we devote attention to figuring out whether we're in the fast one. We run Time-Value calculations in our heads: Is the line with a lone stay-at-home mom and an overflowing cart faster than the express line with five shoppers? When there is only one line, in contrast, it allows attention to wander to other things, perhaps to an iPhone game or telephone call, and the felt time decreases.

Valuations of time vary as well; the same activity may be viewed differently by different people. For an amateur chef, preparing a meal is a highly valued exercise in close attention to detail. For a single working mother, however, meal preparation on a weekday evening is an inconvenience dominated by rote actions that can be absentmindedly fulfilled while she drills one child for a spelling quiz and moderates a shouting match between two others.

By understanding the customer's propensities to spend time and attention and where the breakpoints reside, executives can better develop, customize, target, and market their products in a way that results in a favorable Time-Value Tradeoff. The Time-ographics Framework (see Figure 1–2) helps make the time-and-attention barrier explicit and provides a view into where opportunities lie (and where failures are almost certain).

Customer Time-ographics Analysis

The X-axis of the Time-ographics Framework represents the customer's propensity to spend time on an activity or product, and the Y-axis of the framework represents the customer's propensity to allocate attention to the same.[15] Customer activities—and the products that correspond to

Time-ographics Framework

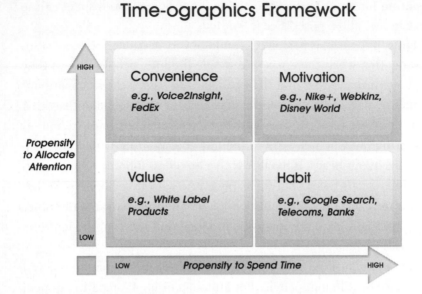

Figure 1–2: The Time-ographics Framework differentiates how customers allocate their time and attention among different products and services.

those activities—thus fall into one of four quadrants: motivation, habit, convenience, or value.

In the upper right of the framework is the motivation quadrant. This is where customers willingly devote considerable time and attention. It is the quadrant where most traditional marketers have sought to position their products and gain emotional attachment. The Nike+ is a motivation-driven product for runners who want to track their performance. Disney World and many Disney products also fall into this quadrant for families. The devotion of time and attention finds its cause in any number of motivations, from the desire for peer and family connection, to power and social status, to personal pursuits (fun, job training, self-improvement).

Despite the desirability of this quadrant, there are simply not enough hours in the day for customers to give all products this level of attention and time. Marketers have focused their efforts on achieving this nirvana without considering a customer's 24-hour constraint. How many products would you place in this quadrant relative to all the other products and services that you purchase and consume? Not only is it difficult to establish products in this coveted and crowded motivation-driven world, it is even more difficult to sustain a position here. Motivations change and shift over time. Once a personal goal is met, interest wanes, or a life-stage is passed, people move in a new direction and leave their old motivations behind.

Habits lie in the lower right-hand quadrant. Here, customers may spend a lot of time, but they are not paying attention. That low level of attention is paid because habitual behaviors reside in the unconscious mind. Autopilot kicks in as people go through their morning routine, or drive to work along the same route they always use.

Research conducted by USC professor Wendy Wood and others estimates that about 45 percent of people's behavior is spent in repetitive and unthinking activities.[16] Many of our frequent purchases are habits as well. A study conducted by the U.K. grocer J Sainsbury showed that even though grocery stores stock tens of thousands of items, shoppers tend to buy from a selection of the same 150 items every week.[17] The habit quadrant also includes systematized background processes that are set to fulfill automatically. An example here is an automatic subscription renewal that is placed on a credit card, or a business process that is ingrained into the procedures and systems of an organization. The habit quadrant delves into the unconscious mind and institutional memory. As you will see in later chapters, the steps to success in this quadrant turn many traditional marketing paradigms upside-down.

The convenience quadrant resides in the upper left corner of the Time-ographics Framework. Here customers dedicate their attention, but only for a short amount of time. Indeed, one of the nuances of convenience is that attention is often dedicated *in the service* of time saving. Convenience stores, fast-food restaurants, and expedited delivery services like FedEx are perhaps the most notable business models designed specifically to address this quadrant. Newer Internet and mobile models are emerging to save customers even more time. In this quadrant, customers are devoting attention, but not necessarily to the product's features or prices; they are concerned with saving time.

On the opposite end of the spectrum from the motivation quadrant is the value quadrant, where customers spend as little time and attention as possible. Products that reside here either possess standard features or have differences that can be compared with little to no thought. Thus customers make decisions that are almost exclusively price driven. Some value-driven product suppliers thrive in this area. Consumer packaged-goods suppliers of "white label" products, for example, make significant profit selling huge volumes of unbranded commodity goods wholesale to large retailers. Walmart and Southwest Airlines are branded examples of companies that have been wildly successful using a value-driven approach. Although some businesses have cost structures designed for this quadrant, many companies that land in the value quadrant do not want to be there and actively seek ways to escape.

Time-Value Tradeoffs and Time-ographics analysis provide fresh ways to view customers in line with today's realities. This mindset offers the opportunity to uncover white-space market opportunities that may be overlooked through traditional means. These methods also provide ways to increase the success of existing products by understanding product adoption barriers and opportunities across the value chain.

Customer Behavior Trumps Attitude

For some readers, this time-and-attention overview may beg the question: What is the difference between Time-ographics analysis and more traditional customer-segmentation methods, such as psychographics? Can't a person's willingness to spend time and attention be categorized within a personality framework?

In my view, the answer to the latter is no. Psychographic definitions often refer to a customer's particular tastes. As a result, they are often attitudinal and static. Personality traits and preferences produce such labels as "environmentalist" or "urban chic" in which the segment is viewed as unchanging depending on the situation. Time-ographics, in contrast, is more about behaviors that drive action at particular points in time rather than general attitudes and tastes. Behavioral considerations tend to be different from personality characteristics—your customers can say they like your product, but if it does not score advantageously in the Time-Value Tradeoff they are not going to find a place for it within their busy lives. Although attitudinal segmentation is still useful, Time-ographics offers a complementary behavioral and situational view of customers.

The good news is that new technologies in the Internet and mobile arenas enable better measurement and understanding of customer behavior in relation to time and attention. Attitudinal methods such as psychographics were originally designed for a mass-market world when it was difficult, if not impossible, for anyone but the big-name brands to measure customer behavior. Today, electronic behavioral targeting and feedback tools are accessible to small businesses as well as the largest corporations.

In the second half of this chapter we will look at the different ways businesses can use the Time-ographics Framework for product innovation and marketing. But before we get there, it's crucial to understand a bit more deeply how the human brain perceives, controls, manages, and reacts to time and attention. As I mentioned, not all time is equal, and it is influenced in part by our brain's inner chemistry, or the unconscious, as well as by the conscious attempts we make to allocate attention and time in our every day.

The Brain and Attention

A customer's propensity to allocate attention is affected by several factors, including attention capacity, the amount and type of information (e.g., attentional blink), and stress.

One does not need a PhD in neuroscience to know that there are limits to our attention. Psychological studies have estimated that human brains can absorb up to 126 bits of information per second, and listen at about 40 bits per second.[18] That's about one to four words a second.[19]

Consider that a high-speed broadband connection transfers, in contrast, between 64,000 and 2,000,000 bits per second. It is sobering to think that all the information we can absorb in a lifetime can be transferred over the Internet in slightly more than a day—the equivalent of 28,032 audio books at listening speed.[20]

Of course, people are not machines. Computers run software that provides a complete set of instructions that run in their entirety every time the machine executes a program. We humans, in contrast, take shortcuts to conserve our limited capacity to pay attention. Our brains employ pattern recognition so as to focus only on things that fall outside the pattern—the new detour sign on our route to work, for example, or the sound of birdsong outside the window on those first mornings of spring. Patterns make it so that we do not have to relearn actions each time we do them. Instead we rely on routines and repeat behaviors to get through most of our days.

For situations that are variable, our brains are expert at identifying and filtering out all unnecessary inputs, such as extraneous sounds or visuals. Psychologists call this the "cocktail party effect," because it allows us to stand in a room of talking people and filter out the speech of everyone except the person we are talking with. Yet when they are important, our brains let extraneous inputs in, such as when our name is mentioned in an adjacent conversation.

Our brains' ability to filter relevant information quite literally keeps us sane. Imagine if every piece of information presented in your day were given equal attention. You would not be able to function. Our cognitive shortcuts help us—though they are not without consequences. The phenomenon of attentional blink that I mentioned in the introduction is one example of how our brains need a second to process after being confronted with an important input, during which no other information can get through.

Another gap our brains create as the result of filtering unnecessary information is called "change blindness." In an experiment conducted by Simons and Levin of the University of Illinois, research participants were asked to give directions to a construction worker on the street. While the two people were talking, two other construction workers walked between them carrying a door-sized piece of wood, thus momentarily blocking their view of each other. Approximately half of the subjects did not notice that a different worker, wearing different-colored clothes and with a distinctly different voice, replaced the original person. The subject kept talking as if nothing had changed.[21]

Stress also has a curious effect on the brain's attention capacity. Short-lived stress caused by an immediate deadline increases the ability to pay attention for a short period of time—this kind of stress improves performance for many people. But long-term systemic stress can cause people to resort to unconscious behaviors and routines.

In one set of experiments described in the journal *Science*, Nuno Sousa and his colleagues at the University of Minho, in Portugal, found that rats that were chronically stressed engaged in rote responses, such as compulsively pressing a bar for food they had no intention of eating. The regions of the brain associated with conscious decision-making and goal-directed behaviors had shriveled, while brain sectors associated with habit formation thrived.[22]

The cocktail party effect, attentional blink, change blindness, and stress response all point to the ways in which our brains attempt to focus our attention only on what is relevant or necessary at the moment, and block out irrelevant inputs. While these concepts are known in neuroscience and psychology, they have been applied inconsistently in everyday life. For every sensible approach taken to reduce the demand on attention (such as standard positioning of gas and brake pedals in cars, or universal traffic signs), there are dozens of counterproductive applications that confound the brain's efforts at efficiency. For example, when a software company delivers a new version of its application with all the core functionality rearranged in different tabs, customers are forced to relearn how to do tasks they thought they had mastered. Such companies actually give customers a much more negative experience than the product developers realize.

Consider the implications of these factors, individually and collectively, on the success of your product, services, and marketing strategies. The time and money spent to relaunch a "new-and-improved" product could fall into the gap of change blindness for more than half of your customers, or frustrate those who don't wish to devote attention to learning a new process. Your effort to capture a new customer segment may fall flat on an overstressed, routine-driven population.

The Brain and Time

Just as the brain allocates its attention resources, it also plays a role in how we perceive and use the time we have available. It's obvious that time passes more quickly when we are doing something we enjoy, but time perception is not always so straightforward. The reality is that we cannot trust our brains when it comes to time. Several factors affect a customer's propensity to spend time, including time perception, time preference, time constraints, and trigger events.

Time Perception: Why Grandma Spends Hours in the Casino

The conscious brain is a crude instrument for telling time. We have watches, clocks, calendars, and appointment reminders in our homes and offices because we can't accurately measure time's passage just by thinking about it. Internally, our circadian rhythms signal when we need to eat or sleep by making us feel hungry or tired, but without external aids, we wouldn't know the hour, the day, or even the year.[23]

Dopamine is an important neurotransmitter, also associated with pleasure and addiction, which scientists have linked with basic time-interval regulation. Warren Meck, a psychology and neurology professor at Duke University, trained rats to recognize specific intervals of time by giving them food only when they pressed a lever after a certain amount of time had passed. The researchers then damaged an area of the brain where dopamine plays a role, and found the rats could no longer judge time intervals.[24] When the rats were administered synthetic dopamine, time interval perception was restored.[25]

Brain researchers suggest that addicted users may be seeking the exhilaration or rush of dopamine (among other brain chemicals) through-out their brain instead of the illegal drug or addictive activity.[26] The role that dopamine plays in addiction has led researchers to explore whether media use registers neurologically as pleasure.[27] Why do users go look-ing for one piece of information on the Web only to get sidetracked by article after article?[28] One theory presented by neuroscientist Jaak Pank-sepp is that people receive the same kind of stimulation from searching the world of ideas that they get from addictive behaviors or substances—what he calls *seeking*.[29] This research suggests that pleasure—even ab-stract pleasure—corrupts our already-impaired perceptions of time.

Sadly, our sense of time's passage worsens as we age. The research of psychology professor Peter A. Mangan shows that the older we get, the more we underestimate the passage of time, even when we are con-centrating on it. In one experiment, Mangan separated individuals into groups by age (19–24 years, 50–60 years, 70–80 years) and then asked each group to estimate three minutes by counting seconds (e.g., 1, 1000, 2, 1000, 3, 1000). The older the group, the more they underestimated time's passage. Keeping participants busy with a task made everyone's estimate worse, with the oldest participants faring the worst.[30] This re-search suggests that everyone, young and old alike, loses track of time, particularly when distracted.

Put together, this material shows that humans are poor at conscious-ly perceiving time, and that those poor perceptions get worse with age and when engaging in a pleasurable or addictive activity. No wonder casinos mask time by removing clocks and covering windows. Now we know why Grandma likes to spend so much time pulling one-armed bandits at the casino—her financial-reward-seeking behavior coupled with her age-and-environment-impaired time perception make the hours fly.

Apply this as well to the concept of the buying-time limitations we discussed at the beginning of this chapter, and it becomes clear that speed is not necessarily the only way to win with busy customers. Time perception can be context specific—some situations compel customers to spend more time, even lose track of it, while others make them so time-aware that they want to spend as little as possible.

Time Preference: Why Some Children
Enjoy the Dentist

Another important element of the propensity for spending time is the customer's preference for or aversion toward spending time with a product. Sometimes this is straightforward (most would rather be someplace other than a dentist's chair), and sometimes it is nuanced (consumers may willingly shop for a new car, but grudgingly shop for, say, groceries).

There are many opportunities to take advantage of time-based attitudes. For example, a person's natural aversion to the dentist may encourage a dentist to find ways to reduce the average visit time. A convenient location helps. So may faster drills, fast-drying adhesives, and quick fluoride treatments. A convincing chair-side manner may even get patients to come in for their six-month cleanings with the argument that more frequent short visits will reduce the need for dramatic interventions.

Alternatively, a dentist may alter the customer experience by making it more distracting. When my children were young, they visited a pediatric dentist whose waiting area featured video games and a two-level climbing castle full of toys. Stuffed animals (and, later, flat-screen TVs) were mounted on the ceiling so the time spent in the chair was more entertaining and less stressful. Although it is hard to believe, my children actually couldn't wait to go to the dentist.

Time preference can guide companies to new and effective ways to position their products. It helps to ask whether consumers view the product as something they want to spend time with or something they want to be done with.

Time Constraints: Why Products Work
in Some Settings but Not Others

My firm, Exponential Edge, once conducted a study for a client in which we tested a new consumer durable product concept in various settings to see what channel offered the best opportunity. We tested it in Internet, grocery store, superstore, and mall settings. At the outset, my client thought that the best place for his offering was at the front of the store near the checkout counters, but my firm's study found that placing the product there would have sounded the death knell. As one participant stated, "Once I hit that checkout counter I want to get out of the store as quickly as possible. I've got my kids in the cart. I don't want to waste time looking at anything."

That same respondent later said that she would have more time to consider the product if it were on display near the pharmacy, where she would see it while waiting for her prescription, or in a mall, where she might have time to consider it. Another respondent said, "I would buy this over the Internet in the comfort of my home, where I can learn about it with a cup of coffee in my hand." These responses demonstrate that time constraints and time setting play a big role in product success. This feedback factored into the ultimate design of the product, which is now doing very well in the market.

Time alternatives, as we discussed in the introduction, are closely related to time constraints. If we have many alternative uses for a time slot, we may forgo an activity altogether in favor of something that is a higher priority. Determining how your product rates against other alternatives at a particular point in time is an important factor.

Trigger Events Drive Purchasing Behavior

Academic researchers have long identified that a trigger or spark is necessary to prompt people to take action. Professor Emeritus R. J. Rummel described this in the 1970s by saying that "a spark, a catalyst, a moment of truth ever seem ready to disrupt our routines . . . We suddenly grasp a need for change."[31]

The role of triggers has become increasingly important to purchase decisions in today's time-starved economy. The never-ending to-do lists and impending deadlines result in more reactive behavior. With so many options vying for attention, a strong trigger is often required to bring a situation to the surface of immediate priority rather than festering in the depths of annoyance and disregard. Critical questions to ask are "When is the customer thinking about the problem that your product addresses?" and "What events are strong enough to prompt the customer to take action?"

Triggers can come from a large external event such as a manufacturing recall or new government rules. A personal situation can also function as a trigger, as when a neighbor buys a new car or a colleague gets a promotion, thus prompting change from the status quo. Such trigger events can cause consumers to reprioritize their schedule and redirect time toward product adoption or defection. Triggers can be invoked by your company and by your competitors, such as price discounts, product usage, and poor call-center-related experiences. As we will see in the drill-down chapters on the Time-ographics quadrants, the types of triggers that drive behavior vary across quadrants.

The Wired Brain: Multitasking

I have focused up to this point on the uncontrollable dynamics that drive our allocations of attention and time. But there are also things we do consciously in an effort to further conserve our brain resources. One of our primary techniques is multitasking. We put in that weekly phone call to mom while in line at the grocery store, for example, or we update our LinkedIn profile while watching the evening news.

The integration of media into everyday lives has dramatically increased our impulse to do more things at once. Researchers at the Council for Research Excellence (CRE) found that U.S. adults spend an average of eight-and-a-half hours a day looking at screens (TVs, PCs, cell phones, and other devices), with more than five of those hours spent in front of the television. Almost half (48 percent) of that screen time is spent engaging in simultaneous activities.[32] Concurrent use of different media, otherwise known as media multitasking, is rampant.

Multitasking at first glance seems like a good way to save time. Who wouldn't want to accomplish two or even three things at once? Unfortunately, it doesn't seem to work out that way. Some activities, such as listening to music while exercising, are suited to simultaneity, but these are the exception. For active thoughts, our brains need focus. Numerous studies have shown that when we try to do two things at once, our brains switch between mental tasks. Rather than parallel process the way a computer does, our brains produce a bottleneck as we reset from one task to focus on the other. The result is that time and attention are lost.[33] While we want to believe that our customers are paying attention as they consider our products or read through our websites, they are more distracted than ever.

Multitasking and Time

Doing two things "at once" can in fact take longer than finishing one task and then moving on to the other. David E. Meyer, director of the Brain, Cognition, and Action Laboratory at the University of Michigan, has shown that multitasking can actually double or triple the amount of time it would take to complete multiple activities sequentially.[34] Psychologist René Marois of Vanderbilt University showed the mechanism behind the time loss with a study involving Functional Magnetic Resonance Imaging (fMRI) scans of the multitasking brain. Multitasking leads to lost time because it forces the brain to process and respond to several competing stimuli at once.[35] The more complex, unfamiliar, and detailed the task, the more time it takes to adjust and the more time is lost.

This is not to say that all multitasking is a drain on time. In fact, humans handle certain multitasking combinations well, particularly when they require engagement by different areas of the brain—cooking and watching television, for example, or driving and listening to the radio. These combinations allow for "true" multitasking because they tap into different brain processes—one requires the brain to process language, while the other relies on practiced motor skills.

A body of research suggests that women are more able than men to manage multiple real-world activities such as those described above. Some say that real-world multitasking may have biological origins, since women needed to care for their children while searching for food or collecting water. Whether this is true or not is open for debate and further research. What we do know is that the role of technology in modern life essentially obliterates any gender advantage. Both men and women are equally bad at media multitasking, particularly when the media is dealing with disparate topics.[36]

Multitasking and Attention

When I say that both men and women are bad at multitasking, I mean that it not only costs time, as described above, but that it drains attention. David E. Meyer from the University of Michigan says that errors increase dramatically when people try to perform two or more related tasks at the same time.[37] Scrolling through email during business lunches and punching out text messages during meetings can kick in our dopamine-reward system, says Meyer, unleashing a pleasure-inducing hit that for an estimated 6 percent of Internet users has become clinically addictive.[38] This suggests that fueling the addiction further diverts attention, increasing the odds of error.

Stanford researchers Professor Clifford Nass, Eyal Ophir, and Professor Anthony Wagner measured the impact of multitasking in a study that compared the accuracy with which "light" and "heavy" multitaskers could identify shapes on a screen. "Heavy" multitaskers were those who tended to engage in five or six media activities at the same time—for example, emailing while instant-messaging, writing a document in Word, watching a sport on television, and following the game on the Web. Light multitaskers tended to use only one or two media at one time. Study subjects were asked to identify the positions of red triangles flashed on a screen—different shapes in other colors were flashed as well, but the subjects were instructed to ignore them.

Heavy multitaskers failed horribly at identifying the red triangles relative to light multitaskers, even in tests during which they were not multitasking. According to Professor Nass, the heavy multitaskers tended to be attracted to irrelevant information more often than light multitaskers.[39]

Multitasking and Age

The impact of multitasking on time and attention affects everyone, though some more than others. Young adults seem to lose less time and attention in switching activities than older adults or children. One theory is that their strong memory capability allows them to store the previous activity until it is resumed. Functional Magnetic Resonance Imaging (fMRI) scans also show that the area of the brain responsible for switching between tasks matures last and deteriorates first. Thus, young children and people over 60 will typically have the most difficulty effectively multitasking.[40]

That won't stop them from trying, though. A study by Burst Media indicated that almost 80 percent of women over 55 engage in media multitasking, compared with 87 percent of 25- to 34-year-olds.[41] A large study by CRE found similar results. Although Baby-Boomers and seniors are adept at many things, the studies suggest that unfortunately multitasking is not one of them. Innovating products for these groups should take these limitations into account.

Capturing the Time-and-Attention Opportunity

We now know that there is a time-and-attention challenge that limits the opportunities for companies seeking to stay competitive and relevant with customers. We know as well that customers engage in subconscious and conscious actions that further skew their perceptions of time and allocations of attention. Armed with this knowledge, we can begin to apply the Time-ographics Framework and analysis. This involves two thought exercises:

1. **Evaluate the context** by mapping your **products** onto the Time-ographics Framework and analyzing **customer activity** from a time-and-attention perspective.
2. **Identify opportunities** that emerge from the framework and customer activity flow.

The Time-ographics Framework and analysis can be applied in several beneficial ways. It helps to identify new product opportunities, or identify actions that deepen market penetration of existing products.

Map the Product

The first use of the Time-ographics Framework involves mapping the company's existing or planned product onto the framework. Careful here! This is not about how much time and attention your company *wants* people to invest in the product; this is about the time and attention the customers have a real propensity or ability to invest based on their priorities associated with this activity. Although there are usually many purchasing factors, in what quadrant is the primary center of gravity for the customer? Does your product reside in multiple quadrants depending on the customer? If so, take note, as you will want to refer to this later. These are customer segments. In which quadrant do the majority of customers use a given product? Although there are a number of factors in purchase decisions, where is the center of gravity for customers?[42] Which quadrant has the product development, marketing, and sales efforts been targeting?

Considering the placement of products in relation to other products will yield important insights. Where do your products stand relative to your competitors? How entrenched is your competitor? Are your competitors' customers in a habit or embedded process? Chapter 7 provides more details, nuances, and how-to's on this mapping exercise.

Map the Customer Activity

The next step in evaluating the context is to evaluate the customer activity in relation to the product. As I've already mentioned, some activities are naturally suited to certain quadrants. Dedicated family activities are almost always going to be motivational, for example, whereas the time spent commuting is almost always going to be habitual.

One useful thought exercise that can help companies identify their customers' propensities for time and attention with activities is to create a customer *context timeline*. A context timeline identifies the time boundaries associated with a particular activity. Companies can create a context timeline by asking these questions: How much time does the customer spend on a particular activity? How often? What is keeping her from investing more time? What might make her invest less? What are the time boundaries beyond which she will not spend more or less? Is she distracted when she is engaged in the activity? What other activities does she engage in before, after, or at the same time as this activity? Does this activity belong in a larger series of actions toward a particular goal (weight loss, for example)?

Another exercise is to determine trigger events that could change or influence behavior relative to your product. They can range from life change events, to system downtime, to poor customer services, to keeping up with the Joneses. Triggers are anything that would cause a customer to seriously consider alternatives.

Once a company knows the customer context as it relates to a particular activity, a follow-on thought exercise is to identify *competing activities* battling for the same slice of time. Is the customer choosing between exercising and meeting friends for coffee or getting a few extra hours of sleep? In general, this exercise involves identifying the major alternative activities that a customer could pursue—and that prospective customers may be engaging in today.

Another consideration at this stage is assessing the customer's simultaneous attention span. Is the customer doing something else at the same time, i.e. multitasking? Is she engaged with other brands/products? If so, which ones? How many simultaneous technologies are in use? (Is the TV on while surfing the Internet?) Does this present opportunities similar to those of the iPod and Nike? Is the customer feeling stressed about time? Is the offer complex, requiring attention, or is it easy to understand?

One nuance that the *context timeline* and *competing activities* exercises may bring forward is that certain activities will occupy multiple quadrants depending on the customer. Let's take two runners and call them Jane and Linda. Jane runs every Tuesday, Thursday, and Saturday, but that is the only routine thing about her running. She is always mixing up her routes and workouts. Sometimes she heads to a local track to do speed work; sometimes she takes a standard route and adjusts it with added hills or calisthenics. She participates when she can in local races, and aims to maintain or improve her personal records. Jane is, in short, a motivated runner. She dedicates significant time and attention to gaining personal improvement and satisfaction from the time she spends pounding pavement.

Linda also runs every Tuesday, Thursday, and Saturday, but that is where the similarity ends. Every time she heads out, Linda runs for the same amount of time along the same route, with no variation. She does not run with another person. She does not particularly care about her times. She does not enter races. Linda may have started running years before to alleviate stress from her job or to maintain her weight, but the original motivation—if there ever really was one—was weak and has long gone. Now, running is a habit. She spends sufficient time every week doing it, but it does not command much of her attention, and she almost never thinks about it unless she is . . . well . . . running.

A company that sells running shoes, or sports apparel or heart-rate monitors, for example, may go through the *context timeline* and *competing activities* exercises and find that their customer base is split among Janes and Lindas. That's okay. Once a company knows generally in which quadrants its customers reside, it is then time to do some hard thinking. Where do the *majority* of customers lie? Where do *repeat* customers lie? What portion of revenue, cost, and profit can be attributed to each of the quadrants?

One can imagine that something along those lines happened at Nike in 2004. The company knew that people were running, since Nike itself had ridden the wave of the sport's increased popularity since the 1970s. It knew as well that many runners liked listening to music but were not satisfied with the experience of traditional music players. Finally, it knew that the most dedicated runners, Nike's best customers, are religious about recording data about their performance.

A brainstorming session focused on Linda would never have resulted in the Nike+. But it might have resulted in a service that charged her credit card and delivered her a new pair of shoes on a fixed cycle. Linda thinks so little about running, you see, that an effort to wake her up to it is just as likely to result in a shift to step aerobics—and a brand change to Reebok—as it is to increase shoe sales, so it is just as well to simply build services into her habit.

Jane, on the other hand, is the right customer for the Nike+, or any other product that easily facilitates her interest in improving her performance. By imagining her and what she might need, Nike hit on a clear product win.

Identify Opportunities

Once the customers' activities have been mapped with corresponding products, you can use the Time-ographics Framework in a third way: to engage in future planning, either of new products or of new customer segments.

Useful questions include: Are there any activity clusters, or things that people tend to do either simultaneously or in close succession? Are there any need gaps or "white space" opportunities—either space between sequential activities or ways to help improve what people are already doing? Are there opportunities to help people save time or attention in a product category best suited to convenience? Can new habits be created?

Mapping products and activities with the customers' propensity for time and attention may reveal some incongruities. For example, a company may be investing in a massive development and marketing effort to up-sell its existing Linda-like customer base on a product best suited to Jane. Or their product development process may have yielded an utterly "cool" product that requires significant attention from the customer to use, while the customer base is sitting in the habit quadrant. This misunderstanding of how much time and attention customers dedicate to particular products is arguably a primary cause of product failure and wasted marketing dollars, and it is manifest everywhere.

Take a commercial I saw recently for a sandwich spread. In an attempt to woo Millennials and increase the coolness factor, the company aired an advertisement playing underground music showing young hipsters partying with the spread (a motivation quadrant approach). Several comments on Internet blogs declared the advertisement "stupid." This is sandwich spread after all. The advertisement prompted comedian Stephen Colbert to create a video parody defending mayonnaise as superior to this spread. The parody highlighted college party antics with beer kegs, declaring the "Mayo-lution!" Although the ad attracted some attention, it was not the right kind of attention. By tying its marketing to a motivation position without a plan to address the product's natural appeal to the convenience, habit, or value quadrant, the company will at best create an unsustainable fad based on 15 minutes of fame. To paraphrase a popular epigram: Mr. Wanamaker would know which half of his marketing budget was wasted.

Opportunities: Time Shifts and Attention Gaps

It might seem at first glance that the motivation quadrant is where all companies want to be, since this is where customers willingly commit time and attention. Unfortunately, things are a bit more complicated than that. It is true that we put the greatest investments of our hearts and minds in the things that motivate us—we want so badly to be good parents and to succeed as professionals, to be desired by our spouses or lovers. But feelings are very volatile here. Noble efforts fail, life-stages pass, things that seemed so important at one point seem petty at another. Motivations, in short, are unstable. Companies that started in the motivation quadrant as a way to capture customers may find that to keep them, they might have to move somewhere else.

This is true not only of motivation-driven offerings. In many cases, the quadrant best suited for market entry is not always the best place to stay for market sustainability. Motivation-driven offerings are hard to sustain; true conveniences can be more oriented to one-off opportunistic selling. Habits *become* habits through repeat use. Many products that initially create a position in the motivation or convenience quadrant may fall back to earth in the value quadrant as the product becomes more familiar or competition increases.

In short, it may be necessary to shift a customer from one quadrant to another in regard to how that customer uses your product. This shift could be actively engineered, or it could happen naturally. Consider a product that starts in the motivation quadrant and then shifts to the habit quadrant. That turns a potentially unstable relationship into a mutually beneficial marriage. Understanding transitions through the framework provides a proactive approach to building a sustainable market position and determining customer priorities.

So far we have explored how time factors into customer decision-making through the Time-Value Tradeoff. We have also discussed how customers prioritize products based on time and attention constraints and introduced the Time-ographics framework. It is amazing to consider how many businesses fail to address customer time and attention when such factors are so integral to customer decisions today. Because few companies have pursued this in a systematic way, executives that pursue a Customer Time-Value mindset for their business will likely discover many fertile opportunities. As we saw in the case of Ty's Beanie Babies, those that wait may find themselves locked out of the market by the competition.

You may be wondering at this point: How do I apply these approaches? The next chapter provides a road map for turning a Customer Time-Value mindset into market traction. I'll also highlight new time- and attention-centric innovation strategies and tools that help you apply the new rules to your business.

CHAPTER 1: TWO-MINUTE TAKEAWAYS

Despite a 24/7 economy and a dramatic proliferation of products, the amount of time customers devote to purchasing has remained constant since the 1960s. Yet consumers today are more distracted by technology. There is a time barrier *and* an attention barrier. For a product to fare well in this environment, the customer will need to perceive a positive **Time-Value Tradeoff**, in which the value to the customer exceeds the total combination of price and time investment.

Applying the new rules enables companies to offer a beneficial Time-Value Tradeoff. The new rules are:

- *Capture* opportunities that emerge from multitasking and distraction.
- *Differentiate* on customer time priorities.
- *View* customers as situational: e.g., behavioral time preferences and triggers.
- *Grow* by shifting time boundaries.
- *Focus on* customer time to evaluate, set up, and consume a product.
- *Create* advantage through customer inertia and time-relevant value.

The **Time-ographics Framework** offers a situational view of the customer to reveal opportunities to apply the new rules. Time-ographics present a customer's propensity to spend time in relation to his or her propensity to pay attention, so that products are prioritized in one of four time-and-attention-based quadrants: motivation, habit, convenience, or value. This framework also includes an analysis of the customer context to identify white-space opportunities and product adoption challenges.

2

CUSTOMER TIME-VALUE
INNOVATION TOOLS
AND STRATEGIES

"Customers constantly triage their mind, time, and dime."
ADAPTATION OF SAM HORN'S QUOTE, "ENTREPRENEURS MUST
CONSTANTLY TRIAGE THEIR MIND, TIME AND DIME"

Silicon Valley legend and video gaming pioneer Trip Hawkins saw an opportunity to revolutionize the video game industry. Most people associate video games with the violent, testosterone-driven war games played in multi-hour blocks by highly caffeinated teenage boys. But Trip, one-time founder of gaming giant Electronic Arts (EA), has created a different kind of product for a different market. His latest venture is Digital Chocolate Inc., a mobile gaming provider whose products—fun, high-quality games that run on the iPhone and other mobile platforms—take minutes to play in small slices of time between activities. Instead of playing for hours at home in the living room, Digital Chocolate customers can play in minutes on the commuter rail platform while they wait for their train, or in the car while waiting in line at the drive-thru. The tagline? "Seize the Minute!"

Trip sees Digital Chocolate as part of a newer movement in gaming. For years, the industry mirrored the path followed by film, whose development long concentrated on improving quality and fidelity around storytelling and production. In gaming, this manifested in a generation of products whose value was tied to high-quality graphics and elaborate narratives. The traditional gamer may still want that, but there is a whole category of customers today that is motivated to play fun, short games that employ simple designs and facilitate social interactions— serving as a grist mill to talk with friends. Trip views Digital Chocolate's games, as well as properties like Guitar Hero and many games for the Wii, as part of this newer movement.

"The graphics on the Wii are very simple, but people don't care," Trip says. "It is popular because the Wii is about getting Junior out of the basement and playing the game together with the family in an interactive experience. People want to play games but don't have a lot of time. Rather than pursuing complex, time-consuming sagas, there is a large market out there that is seeking simpler, high-quality games that are fun and don't take hours to play."[1]

Trip and his team utilized a time boundary strategy to "seize the minute," and ultimately opened up a new market segment in gaming. This chapter will explore how time boundary strategies can be utilized to innovate new market opportunities. Shifting time boundaries is one of the new rules for winning in a time-starved, always-connected economy.

Delivering Value by Shifting Boundaries of Time and Attention

In chapter 1, I explored how Time-Value Tradeoff and customer Time-ographics work together within the customers' life and context to define how they prioritize their time-and-attention allocations to products. I outlined as well the ways in which companies can map their product, their customers, and their opportunities within the Time-ographics Framework. That exercise alone may reveal opportunities or shifts that can be applied in the drill-down quadrant chapters that follow. But before we get there, many of you may at this point be asking what can be done about those opportunities. If customers have a time barrier and an attention barrier, what tools are available to shift the constraints in your favor?

What I've discovered is that there are time boundary strategies and tools that actively take into account time-and-attention dynamics. Innovating products with Time-Value in mind can be approached systematically. As depicted in Figure 2-1, you can 1) conduct a Time-ographics analysis of the context and opportunities; 2) assess time boundary strategies and tools that can be applied; and 3) drive product adoption and market traction by applying Time-Value Tradeoffs and tools.

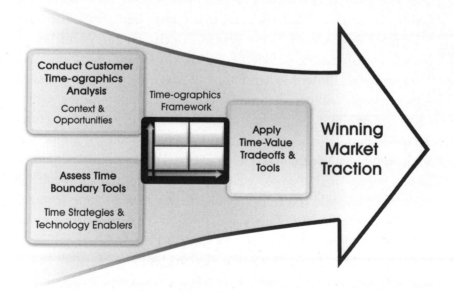

Applying the New Rules
Turning Customer Time-Value into Market Traction

Figure 2–1: The approach: Customer Time-ographics analysis and time boundary strategies provide critical inputs to the framework that uncover market opportunities and identify product adoption requirements. This process results in winning market traction for a new offering.

Active accounting of time-and-attention dynamics is the relevent point here. Business owners have known intuitively for a long time that certain time-and-attention-driven techniques work to convince customers to spend time and money with them. Grocery stores know that keeping checkout lines short will prevent buyers from turning away at the door. Food purveyors in shopping malls know that delicious smells can entice people to stop and buy. Even Web page designers follow the "three-click" rule of thumb, designing their sites so that customers can find content within three clicks of the home page. Such time-saving and attention-capturing techniques have been in practice for a number of years, and they can be very effective.

The challenge for many innovators, however, is that time-and-attention-oriented techniques are deployed more through instinct than through any clear strategy. You do see them, but they are rarely deployed systematically. On the contrary, they are often used contradictorily and in functional silos, resulting in conflicting signals for customers. Short lines may draw people in, but inconvenient parking keeps them out; smells say "come in," but loud, fast music says "hurry up!" The time boundary business methods I present in this chapter are systematic approaches to innovating products by using Customer Time-Value and Time-ographics. Take another look at Digital Chocolate. As a leisure activity, people willingly dedicate time and attention to games, so video games intuitively reside in the motivation quadrant of the Time-ographics Framework. Yet the Digital Chocolate audience segment is adult professionals and parents, nontraditional gamers who don't *have* a lot of time. So Trip has employed a strategy to conform the game to the customer's schedule constraints in such a way that the time required does not destabilize the Time-Value Tradeoff. To reference the equation that we discussed in chapter 1 (Value > Price + Customer Time Investment), he reduced the time needed to play the game, making the tradeoff more attractive to the buyer. He also increased the quality of the games, thus increasing the value of the time spent.

By January 2010, after 12 months of offering games for the iPhone, Digital Chocolate had reached more than 50 million downloads (almost 1 million downloads per week), with six products reaching first place in the Apple App Store. Digital Chocolate has generated close to 2 million user reviews with more five-star reviews than any other company in the gaming category.[2]

In this chapter, let's walk through an overview of some time boundary strategies that are most commonly deployed today. The boundary strategies presented are not mutually exclusive. Certain boundary strategies can be blended together depending on the situation. We will see many of these strategies in action in subsequent chapters when we drill down into specific opportunities that evoke motivations, shape habits, and create conveniences.

Time Boundary Strategies

The tendency of many companies in the current time-and-attention-constrained world is to get louder—to promote more heavily on a broader variety of platforms with a jazzier hook. This might work in some instances, but for most products, an approach that drains more customer time and attention is more likely to annoy and repulse than to attract. There are a host of alternative concepts and techniques out there—many of them low-tech—that create an opportunity for products to slip in and take hold within the boundaries of a person's time-and-attention constraints. Some of these techniques are suited to products that fall in specific quadrants, while others are quadrant neutral. They include techniques that, broadly:

- Increase time value (or decrease time cost)
- Redefine time use
- Shift the purchase and consumption flow

Increase Time Value

Some of the most familiar business methods involve increasing the value of time spent with the customer or reducing the time cost. This can be accomplished by increasing dwell time (the time customers spend with you), instant gratification, ease of use, creating time-critical value, trading customer time for value, and targeting the senses.

Create Dwell Time

Significant research supports the argument that increasing a person's "dwell time," or the amount of time a customer spends in your store or on your website, increases the likelihood that the customer will buy something and that more revenue will be generated. Consulting firm Deloitte has found that customers that use a fitting room in a clothing store buy 85 percent of the time, compared with a 58 percent sales rate among shoppers who did not use the fitting room.[3] A behavioral researcher at Cornell's Food and Brand Lab likewise observed that grocery shoppers that spend time reading labels actually spend more money than those who are rushed.[4] And Path Intelligence, a U.K. company whose technology tracks the footpaths of people by triangulating their cell phones with the cellular network, found that a dwell time increase of 1 percent corresponded with a 1.3 percent sales increase.[5] Major industry players such as Nielsen, ComScore, and Alexa likewise track time spent on websites as a measure of success and ranking.

Retailers have long employed techniques to increase dwell time. Grocers place staple purchases such as milk and bread at the back of the store, requiring that customers walk all the way through—and past something else they might want. They are especially adept at lining this yellow brick road with tempting higher-margin items (such as meat, produce, bakery goods, flowers, and the retailer's own goods) to increase the profitability of the basket/final ring. All of the low-margin items, such as canned tomatoes, are buried in the "box" of the aisles. In the online world, Web retailers employ similar techniques to hold customers on their site, such as curiosity-grabbing "today's deals."

Increasing dwell time not only allows stores to gain probable sales, it also eats into a person's three-hour-a-week shopping time, decreasing the likelihood that the consumer can consider competitive alternatives. The Webkinz case study I shared in the introduction demonstrates this displacement effect. Children were occupied and entertained inside the Webkinz virtual world, leaving little time available for Beanie Babies 2.0 within the time allotted for Internet play. It should be noted that dwell time does not apply in all contexts, nor should it be confused with inefficient execution. Convenience-driven products make their name from speed and efficiency. Jiffy Lube, for example, or one-hour eyeglass shops, or even fast-food restaurants may not find value in increasing customer dwell time (though I'd love to see the conversion rates of retailers located *next door* to the eyeglass shop, who are beneficiaries of that one hour within which the company promises to make your glasses).

Likewise, we may like to linger in a shop admiring the merchandise, but when it is time to buy, we want the purchase transaction to be efficient. No one likes long lines or excessive Web registration processes. It is with this in mind that I differentiate here between *convenient* interactions and the convenience quadrant. Fast, convenient checkout and transactions are expected across all Time-ographics quadrants, whereas convenience quadrant products are about saving time as the main value proposition to the client. A customer may be in the motivation quadrant, but that person still expects customer service at the Porsche dealer to pick up the phone without delay.

The customer's expectation of convenience extends to product set-up and use, as I experienced with the MP3 player discussed in the introduction—such time-wasters factor into the customer Time-Value Tradeoff. With time at a premium and a glut of options available, most consumers will no longer tolerate products that come in pieces and require hours of software installation and manual reviews. Some of the companies that I work with now purposefully design their products up front with a goal to make the product so intuitive that a manual is completely unnecessary. Apple led the way in this area. This should be a design goal for any new product today. Some companies now regularly run market tests to time and observe how long it takes a consumer to unpack the box and set up a new product.

Provide Instant Gratification

When we want it, we want it now. Technology has enabled a compression of the purchasing cycle for many items. Prior to the growth of the Internet, purchases followed discrete steps through time. First, we became aware of a particular need. Then we began gathering information about options to fulfill that need, eventually landing on a preferred product and making a purchase. The amount of time it took to progress through the Awareness-Consideration-Preference-Purchase steps may have been very brief for simple purchases, less so for more complicated items; but still the movement was linear.

Now with the Internet and mobile devices we can access customer reviews and product information, IM our friends for advice while in the store, or use a single click to buy with predefined accounts and credit card information. These tools enable us to transact more quickly. Product delivery can also be near-instant with Web downloads, remote repair services, and overnight delivery. Customer needs, product information, calls to action, and delivery are converging into near simultaneity. What this means is that innovators and marketers must increasingly synchronize customer needs (peaked by trigger events) with the information (product/customer reviews/call to action) and Time-Value Tradeoff of the product to address purchasing windows when they occur (see Figure 2–2).

Deliver Time-Critical Value

Instilling a sense of urgency is a well-tested strategy. Businesses create a "limited time offer" or "good until the 15th" promotion as a way to imply that a good is scarce. Overuse can dilute such tactics, however. Macy's was famous for its "one-day sales," which it advertised to Macy's credit card holders and other preferred customers. But any middle-of-the-week trip to the Macy's department store had a 50:50 chance of falling on one of those sales. Such frequency diminishes the meaning and tells customers they never need to pay full price—they can always wait until the next sale.

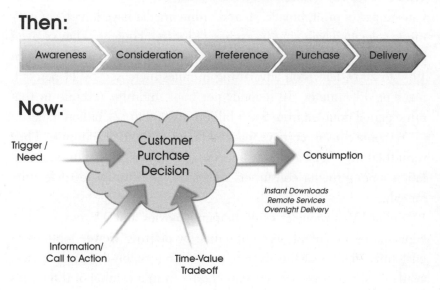

Figure 2–2: Customers who "want it now" require businesses to synchronize the triggered need with product information, call to action, and the Time-Value Tradeoff.[6]

Connecting timing with value can also enable new product of-ferings. For instance, a client came to my firm complaining that his product was viewed as a commodity by his manufacturing customers. After we interviewed a number of customers, we found that his im-pression was accurate during the normal course of business. But when the manufacturer's assembly line failed, creating millions of dollars in potential losses with every hour, the customer was willing to pay a premium for my client's assistance. In response, my client designed assurance products and specialized services to proactively reduce line failure, and bring his customers to normal operation quickly when the lines failed. Designing the product around critical timing trig-gers increased revenue and differentiation in the market. Fixing time-critical problems is another way to deliver high margin value using the new rules.

Trade Time for Value

Consumers of print, broadcast, and online media have long been willing to tolerate advertising in exchange for free content. They've even been willing to tolerate increases in advertising—up to a point. From 1999 to 2009, television advertising minutes increased by 14 percent, reaching 15 minutes, 30 seconds per hour. Industry revenue in that same period doubled from $10.5 billion in 2000 to $21 billion today.[7]

Yet some consumers have reached their threshold of ad inputs. They want their time back and may be willing to pay to get it. This segmentation among media consumers opens an opportunity to trade time for value.

ZillionTV, a provider of on-demand movies and TV programs, is capitalizing on the ad overabundance by offering viewers options to customize their viewing experience.[8] Using an on-demand service, available at any time, viewers can choose from a catalog of thousands of Hollywood movies and TV shows, according to what they want to watch and when they want to watch it. The consumer can also decide whether to watch a show for free with advertisements or on a pay-per-view basis without commercials. For those who choose to watch the ads, ZillionTV viewers can opt to enter profile information into the system so the ads presented can be consistent with their interests and highly relevant. This approach benefits the entire ecosystem—the viewer, the advertiser, and ZillionTV.[9] A separate research study conducted by Comcast Corp. found that viewers watched targeted advertisements 38 percent longer than less-relevant commercials.[10]

Influencing Time and Attention
by Targeting the Senses

The five senses of sound, sight, touch, smell, and taste allow customers to quickly assess a product and can have great influence on a person's propensity for time or attention. Senses also become extremely relevant as people reach the limits of their attention—they can be used as an efficient, unconscious way to engage.

Sound, for instance, has been found to increase and influence sales. Researchers observed that music at a slow tempo in stores can increase sales by 38 percent because its relaxing effect incents shoppers to stick around and spend more.[11] In another study, French music played in a wine store caused 80 percent of shoppers to buy French wine; German music meant more German wine was purchased. The effect seemed unconscious. When asked, only 2 percent of customers stated that the music was the reason they selected the wine.[12]

Sight has long been the focus of advertising. Colors play an important role in sight-sense associations. Warm colors such as reds and oranges are associated with activity, excitement, and gastronomic delight. Cool colors such as greens, purples, and blues are more relaxing. That is why you are more likely to see orange and terra-cotta on the walls of a restaurant, while sage and sea-foam are more frequently used for beauty product packaging.

Touch generates positive product associations. Bookstore customers who were touched on the arm shopped almost twice as long and bought 23 percent more.[13] In this and other studies, respondents evaluated the store more positively than customers who had not been touched.

Warmth and cold also affect human time perceptions. In the 1930s, researcher Dr. Hudson Hoagland found that he could retard an individual's sense of time by applying heat to the brain. Other researchers later found that lowering body temperature by two or three degrees could speed up the subjective sense of time.[14] Although I don't advocate freezing or overheating customers, it does seem that the temperature in a store or service location could affect your customers' willingness to stick around.

Smell strongly affects a shopper's experience. Research confirms that enticing smells increase sale rates. One study found that in a floral-scented room, 84 percent of respondents held more positive feelings about the product than the identical product presented in an unscented room.[15] When Exxon convenience stores in North Carolina deployed coffee scents, coffee sales perked up by a healthy 55 percent.[16]

Individually and together, the five senses create unconscious feelings about product offerings. They offer important cues and feedback that can elicit habit-based, unconscious behavior, and rapidly send signals to the buyer about product quality and capability.

Redefine Time Use

As we saw with Digital Chocolate, a company can take into account time-and-attention constraints by designing and delivering products that will be consumed according to consumer availability. There are four ways to do this: time slicing, time shifting, linking to future time, or taking advantage of captive time.

Time Slice

Time slicing involves designing products that will fit into small gaps of available time, such as the 10 minutes spent waiting for a commuter train to arrive, a prescription to be filled, or a television program to download. Digital Chocolate employs a time-slicing strategy by delivering quick, simple games designed for the iPhone and other platforms that can be played within the available time window.

Another product that survives on slices of time is DailyLit (www. dailylit.com), a company that was formed when the founders realized that they could spend hours reading email but didn't have time to read a book.[17] Rather than designing the product to fit entirely within a time window, DailyLit breaks the product apart into manageable pieces. Adopting the serialization model popular when Charles Dickens was writing classics such as *The Pickwick Papers*, DailyLit cuts books into bite-sized chapters and allows the reader to choose when to receive them. DailyLit delivers chapters via email or RSS feed to the computers and mobile devices of more than 150,000 subscribers.[18]

A variation of time slicing is time sharing. In this case, the product is typically a costly item such as a vacation home that is sliced into digestible, often more affordable pieces and is consumed by many buyers rather than by one. Each purchaser is given a time allocation based on how many shares are purchased.

Avelle (www.bagborroworsteal.com) is a company that bills itself as the "Netflix of purses."[19] Members who sign up for their service rent a designer handbag or accessories for up to a year. The member rents the latest Prada for an evening soiree and then orders a Louis Vuitton accessory for her next event. She never has to sport the same fashion look twice. This service opens up a previously unserved market segment by bringing luxury items within reach of the mid-level consumer.

Time Shift

Time shifting was originally popularized by TiVo digital video recorders (DVRs) that allow viewers to record their favorite TV shows and watch them when it better fits their schedule. Time-shifting hardware has since been joined by content providers such as Hulu and Netflix that make thousands of movie and TV titles available on demand for download or online viewing. Though the term "time shifting" typically refers to delayed viewing of video content, one can view Internet e-commerce as another form of time shifting, since it shifts buying patterns to a time when the customer has availability outside the typical retail business hours. We can expect time shifting to emerge in other industries as well, as new products are innovated using this technique.

Link to Future Time Windows

When businesses proactively create time opportunities in the future to connect with customers, they are linking to a future time window. They accomplish this in one of three ways: 1) scheduling a repeated activity in the future, such as dental hygiene appointments, every six months; 2) providing follow-up from an existing product with perishable replenishment or maintenance needs; or 3) creating cross-platform elements to benefit future products.

Although regularly scheduled appointments have been easy to execute, maintenance or replenishment of items that have varying schedules have not been easy to track or communicate in a time-relevant manner. One product that has been successful in this arena is GM

OnStar. Although General Motors has faced significant issues with profitability and relevance, its GM OnStar unit has provided a silver lining. OnStar's telematic services range from emergency services to turn-by-turn navigation. OnStar also emails the owner every month with diagnostics pertaining to the vehicle. For customers who opt in, OnStar notifies local dealers when a vehicle requires scheduled service. The dealer then contacts the customer to schedule a service appointment. Certain customers appreciate the reminder in lieu of tracking the maintenance status themselves. According to GM, this service can boost service revenue for medium-to-large dealerships up to $15,000 per month.[20]

The third strategy, cross-platform elements, is an evolving tool. It can be used when a product will naturally erode from the customers' attention at some point (usually a motivation quadrant product). To counter this, the company creates a common element that extends across the product line to link to a new motivation quadrant product they introduce.

Consider Digital Chocolate's NanoStars, virtual characters that people can buy that reference popular culture (Octomom) or historical names (Robin Hood).[21] According to Trip Hawkins, "With nearly all virtual items today, customers are buying a single object with limited emotional value that works only in a single game [such as a more powerful sword]. The first big difference is that with NanoStars you are getting a vibrant, [memorable], and emotionally compelling virtual character, not merely an object. The second difference is even more crucial in that NanoStars morph into different things in different games or apps so the customer gets much more for their money and develops a more meaningful relationship. I like to think of it as Pokémon for grownups."

Through NanoStars, Digital Chocolate offers a consistent cross-game connection. A customer who tires of the current game can use the character in a new one. Similar to a loyalty program, the virtual character builds capabilities and powers, creating incentive to stick with a brand, but in a fun, new way.

Leverage Captive Time

Moviegoers waiting for their film to start and passengers waiting for flights are considered "captive" audiences. Airports capitalize on these potential consumers by creating giant shopping malls with brand-name retail stores and upgrading the concessions with higher-quality restaurants. Although the concessionaires make most of the money from this, the revenues are shared with the airports. Finding a quiet place to sit without paying for it is now a rarity.

Professional sports teams are probably the best example of utilizing captive time for profit. On top of pricey game tickets, most game attendees buy the $20 hot dog and beer, and visit the stadium store to acquire team-logoed sports memorabilia. You may recall the classic Master-Card commercial that described this phenomenon by showing a person rack up more than $100 in costs attending a ball game and ending with "Real conversation with your eleven-year-old son? . . . Priceless."

Anywhere customers need to wait presents opportunities for captive time products when executed tastefully and in line with the customers' frame of mind.

Shift the Purchase/Consumption Cycle

As I mentioned before, most companies traditionally operate within the cycle of awareness, consideration, preference, purchase—then consumption. The customer has been attuned to that order of things since the 1950s, but some new products are changing the time boundaries associated with the purchasing process. Newer models include integrating purchase into consumption, and shifting the order of purchase and consumption.

Integrate Purchase into Consumption

As we know, U.S. customers spend only about six minutes a day with e-commerce sites.[22] Given this limited time window with customers, an e-tailer like Amazon.com is faced with two alternatives in the battle for customers:

1. Fight a bloody pricing battle with other e-commerce sites like Barnes & Noble.com and Walmart.com to garner share in the six-minute time window.
2. Go beyond traditional buying processes and integrate with customer consumption activities.

Amazon chose the latter when it launched the Kindle e-reader. Through the Kindle, Amazon not only facilitates the purchase transaction, it actually participates in the customer's consumption activity of reading a book. As a result, Amazon remains with the reader for longer than the standard six-minute buying transaction; the e-tailer serves as a constant customer companion. (see Figure 2–3).

A Tablet/E-Reader Shifts Time Boundaries from a Book Transaction to a Constant Customer Companion

Traditional: Purchase Online, then Consume (separately)

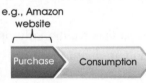

e.g., Kindle E-Reader: Integrates Purchase into Consumption (reading)

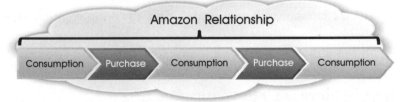

Figure 2–3: Tablets and e-readers increase dwell time and customer inertia by integrating purchasing into the consumption of media.

This new way of servicing the market has expanded Amazon's ability to achieve greater market penetration. An e-reader is right there with an e-commerce link and preloaded user profile information available at the push of a button when a customer buying impulse is triggered—taking much of the guesswork out of predicting when a customer will buy and what website she will choose. Why would Kindle users buy from anyone else when Amazon makes it so easy? Indeed, in 2009 Amazon indicated that users order 2.6 times as many books—both print and e-books—when they purchase a Kindle.[23]

The idea of creating a proprietary ecosystem that integrates product use with add-on purchases is compelling—so much so that Barnes & Noble and Apple are taking on Amazon with their own e-reader/media devices, the Nook and iPad, respectively. The race is on as to who will win the e-reader market. Yet the most important aspect of this market is not the hardware. Hardware is an ingredient in the customer experience. The winner in this market will be the company (Amazon, Barnes & Noble, Google, Sony, Apple, or another) that gains the most customer adoption of the e-reader interface with a direct link to an application (online retail).

The provider that gains the greatest e-reader software market share will hold the default position because that company holds the time and attention of the customer. As a result, the interface owner is in the best position to introduce new value-added services and cross-selling opportunities to those customers. The Time-Value Tradeoff will drive customers to stick with what they know. Owning the time and attention of the customer—via the user interface and default purchasing preferences—is a key way to create competitive advantage under the new rules.

Shift the Order of Purchase and Consumption

With his book *Free*, *Wired* editor Chris Anderson brought significant attention to the way many digital products today attract customers through free services.[24] Although free is a price, it is also a business model. Free, of course, is not really free. Products are usually paid for somehow by somebody. Free models instead often turn this flow on its head by allowing customers to gain value from the product before paying for it. Companies convert revenues in one of three ways:

- By converting a subset of customers to higher-quality paid versions
- By adopting an ad-supported model (i.e. trading time for value)
- By cross-selling other products or affiliate offerings

Examples of "consume first, pay later" models include content sites, such as the *Wall Street Journal* and the *Economist*, that provide some content for free while holding "premium" material for paying subscribers. Personal-finance software provider Intuit also offers free and paid versions of its popular TurboTax tax preparation software, and it cross-sells form review and audit protection services. These approaches alter the entire value chain, from product design (creating free *and* paid versions), to marketing (advertising through trial), to sales (focusing on the few customers who will convert to paid upgrades), to service (possibly a revenue source).

How Time Boundary Strategies and Time-Value Interact

Up to this point we have discussed many of the ingredients that may be combined to develop time- and attention-centric opportunities, namely, time boundary strategies, Time-Value Tradeoffs, and Time-ographics. As a foundation, it is helpful to explain how a few of these ingredients interact to help inform your reading of the upcoming quadrant drill-down chapters (motivation, habit, convenience, value). We cannot change time itself, but time boundary strategies are levers that executives can pull to alter the relationship between a customer's unwillingness to adopt a new product or change behavior because of perceived time constraints.

As we have seen, stress, overwork, and bulging to-do lists often create situations where people tend to resort to sticking with what they know best. Current products and activities usually hold an inertia position for the customer. When given a choice, the status quo will usually prevail unless a Time-Value threshold is exceeded. For example, if you were thinking about switching your account to another bank, you would not only evaluate what the other bank has to offer but would factor in the time and effort it takes to switch. For many customers, the effort of switching banks is so significant that they opt to stay where they are. In fact, only 11 percent of U.S. customers change banks each year.[25]

Although the concept of switching costs is not new, these time-based purchasing factors are nonfinancial in nature. The pain is not from financial loss, but from the perception about the time investment and hassle to switch. The Time-Value Tradeoff is in action.

This relationship is reflected in the conceptual diagram in Figure 2–4. Trigger events (represented by the peaks in lines "A" and "B") increase your receptivity to switch. A small trigger event would occur if you were served by a rude customer service representative. Although you might consider switching, a gap would exist between the new product and your willingness to switch (the difference between the small peaks and the dotted line "New Product or Activity"). However, if your bank accidently lost some of your money, then the big peak would occur ("B") and you would be more receptive to switching immediately. This is how triggers and Time-Value interact.

Companies cannot always wait or create a major trigger event, so shifting time boundaries enables them to acquire new customers. If the bank were to create a very helpful switching kit that would do all the hard work of transitioning an account, reducing time investment (lower dotted line), then the Time-Value line would shift down to where it reaches more trigger points and the Time-Value threshold is reached. At that point, the Time-Value Tradeoff is favorable and the customer would be likely to make the switch.

Understanding triggers and timing, as well as using time boundaries to change the perception of Time-Value, will increase the customer

Shifting Time Boundaries Increases Customer Acquisition Thresholds

e.g., Bank Switch Kits

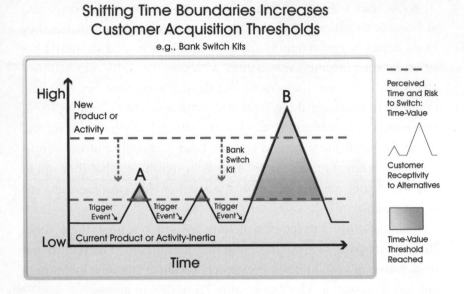

Figure 2–4: Trigger events prompt prospective customers to be more receptive to product alternatives. It is at these points when the Time-Value threshold to switch to a new product is reached. Shifting time boundaries creates more customer acquisition opportunities by reducing the time and hassles of switching.

acquisition rate. This enables companies to focus time and marketing investments for highest return.

Technology Enablers

Many of the methods described throughout this chapter employ technology as an enabler that plays a proactive role in driving customer behavior and creating market traction. It does so by:

- Guiding customer choice through structured online menus, memory cues, and persuasive techniques
- Creating familiar interfaces and stored user preferences that promote user inertia

- Enabling time preference and time-relevant value through customized information
- Developing a rapid innovation platform that enables new products to be developed, thus keeping pace with changing customer tastes and holding customer attention

The next four chapters will drill down into the four quadrants of the Time-ographics Framework, namely: motivation, habit, convenience, and value. We will address each chapter by exploring the triggers that drive customer behavior in the quadrant; how to establish a position in the quadrant; how to sustain a position; and why positions fail for some companies. The time boundary tools and strategies described in this chapter will be applied through case examples in the upcoming chapters.

CHAPTER 2: TWO-MINUTE TAKEAWAYS

There are many time-and-attention-based tools and strategies available to apply a Customer Time-Value mindset to product innovation, marketing, and customer service. In fact, companies have been applying some of these strategies for years—they simply have not been doing it in a systematic way. Some of these tools actively utilize technology. Some are simply the provenance of good Customer Time-Value design.

- *Rule:* Capture opportunities that emerge from multitasking and distraction.
- *Tool:* Time slice to redefine a product to fit within a time window.
- *Rule:* Differentiate on customer time priorities.
- *Tool:* Trade time for value, or provide time-critical value.
- *Rule:* View customers as situational.
- *Tool:* Capture captive time in airports or stadiums.
- *Rule:* Grow by shifting time boundaries.
- *Tool:* Time shift so customers can consume at a later time, or integrate consumption with purchase so the two are enmeshed, or reduce the time investment required to adopt the new product.
- *Rule:* Focus on customer time to evaluate, set up, and consume.
- *Tool:* Evaluate new delivery methods that create instant gratification as a way to change the game. What would it take?
- *Rule:* Create advantage through customer inertia and time-relevant value.
- *Tool:* Utilize dwell time and target the senses so that the customer has no incentive to look elsewhere.

3

TIME MAGNETS:
MOTIVATION QUADRANT
PRODUCTS

*"Give a person a fish and you feed them for a day; teach that
person to use the Internet and they won't bother you for weeks."*
AUTHOR UNKNOWN

In 2005, security and data protection software provider Symantec was
confronting a significant challenge in selling to information technology (IT) departments. Their sales representatives were having difficulty
gaining the attention of senior IT executives. However, they were not
alone in this challenge. According to International Data Corporation
(IDC), corporate IT buyers spend only about 41 minutes a day reviewing outside information from vendors, friends, consultants, industry
authorities, and the media related to current or future technology purchase decisions[1] (see Figure 3–1). Chief information officers often del-
egate the development of vendor "short lists" and technical evaluations
to their subordinates, so their average time spent reviewing vendor information is likely less than the average.

"The IT industry invested $174 billion in 2008 in sales and marketing to reach and influence the IT buyer, yet most executives spend a fraction of their day evaluating purchases," says Clare Gillan, a senior vice president at IDC. "That's a lot of investment chasing a small amount of time."

Symantec had spent years and millions of dollars during the early 2000s transforming itself with new products and acquisitions into a full-service security and risk management software and service provider. Yet most CIOs still associated the company with its original Norton antivirus product. "We had developed tremendous capability in assessing and addressing security and IT risk, yet many customers still held outdated perceptions of us as just an antivirus software company," states Kim Johnston, former vice president of Marketing and Sales Operations at Symantec.

Security and information risk management have become critical

A Day in the Life of an IT Buyer

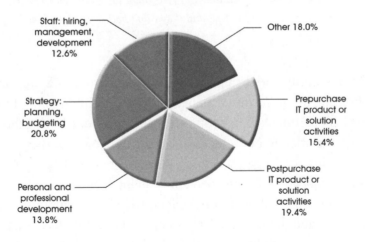

n=296, time is averaged across an entire work year; work peaks and valleys exist
Source: IDC Customer Experience Survey, February 2009

Figure 3–1: IT Buyers spend a fraction of their time on purchasing decisions.

CIO issues, but antivirus software is considered a low-level decision best left to the technical specialists. Understandably, Symantec wanted to escape from the historical view of its products and to position itself as a trusted partner helping companies address IT risk, security, and compliance. Doing so would help its sales reps persuade CIOs to spend time with them.

To overcome the time barrier, the marketing team at Symantec created the INFORM (**INFO**rmation assurance **R**isk **M**odel) Program, a benchmarking tool designed to help CIOs better understand their organization's IT risk. The INFORM program asks CIOs to answer a survey about their security, compliance, and management practices and then compare themselves to other companies. With more than 1,400 companies participating in the INFORM database, the benchmarks can help a CIO see if his or her company is in danger because of lax policies and procedures, or if the company is spending too much money on them. That's information that a CIO will take time to hear.

Johnston says, "Prior to the INFORM program, our sales representatives attempted to call high in the organization, but the CIO was often too busy. Once we launched INFORM, everything changed. Just one example: A global 1000 account that we had been trying to penetrate for several years contacted us, and the CIO gave us all the time and attention we needed to administer and review the benchmarks. We closed a sale of $3 million in three months, not the nine to twelve months it usually takes."

INFORM created a large funnel of sales opportunities, with a 50 percent customer pipeline close rate on leads generated from the program, much higher than the industry average. With rich customer data in hand, Symantec was not only able attract more customers, it also developed detailed reports and analyses that could be shared with customers and the industry, further demonstrating its leadership in IT risk management. The data repository became a rich source of product innovation ideas for Symantec's developers.

Symantec's INFORM program is an example of a motivation offering because it connects with an underlying motivation in a sustainable way. Like a magnet, it creates attraction for CIOs to willingly devote their time and attention. This chapter and the three that follow provide a drill-down into each of the four quadrants of the Time-ographics Framework, specifically: motivation, habit, convenience, and value. In each chapter we will explore the triggers that drive customer behavior in the quadrant; how to establish a position in the quadrant; how to sustain a position; and why positions fail for some companies. Let's further explore the motivation quadrant.

Involving the Heart and Mind

Business executives often say to me, "I want customers to emotionally engage with my brand." Indeed the motivation quadrant often seems like the place to be. However, while it is possible to engage customers emotionally, it is a tall order, and many companies and products simply can't get there for reasons we'll explore throughout this chapter.

The fetishization of emotional connection is easy to understand. Emotional connection means motivated customers, and motivated customers usually mean repeat customers and high margins. What savvy executive wouldn't want that? But to live in the motivation quadrant—not just visit it on the back of a fad, but to really live there—you have to both truly understand the sources of customer motivation and be willing to invest perpetually and richly to stay engaged with those sources.

Motivation offerings appeal to the mind, of course, but they can also appeal to the heart. The mind connection comes from intellectual engagement (such as with a work of literature) or from the potential for improvement (as with a self-help program or a musical instrument). The heart connection comes from our emotional engagement; we feel good when we engage with a particular item or activity, or when a certain brand brings out strong feelings in us. When the level of positive emotional connection with an offering is significant, customers will outwardly refer, recommend, and strongly defend it to other potential buyers. This quadrant is where customers become your marketers and salespeople through word of mouth.

When the heart and mind are engaged, people are compelled to spend more time, sometimes losing all track of it. This effect has been coined as "flow" by psychologist Mihály Csíkszentmihályi. Flow is the mental state a person attains when fully immersed in what he or she is doing. It is a feeling of energized focus, full involvement, and success in the process of the activity.[2]

Three Underlying Triggers That Attract Time and Attention

To tap into the mind and heart appeal of motivational offerings, it is important to understand the psychology behind motivations. Psychological literature is laden with varying definitions of human motivation, and psychological theorists define needs in different ways—intrinsic versus extrinsic motivation, for example—but they all tend to agree that a "need" builds tension or anxiety in a person until that need is met. People minimize anxiety by "steering" toward a way of fulfilling a need.

In the motivation quadrant, trigger events are driven by the heart and mind and create an incentive for people to engage with a particular product or service. There are three underlying motivations that drive high time and attention in this quadrant: 1) peers (family, social camaraderie, physical attraction); 2) power (status and greed); or 3) personal pursuits (self-improvement, curiosity, fun, and fear). Let's explore the triggers that ignite action with these motivations.

Peers

Gaining acceptance with family and friends and avoiding social rejection and loneliness can be strong triggers to action. Common emotions in the family/social motivation include happiness, affection, devotion, loyalty, and love.

Physical attraction is another element of the peer motivation. "Sex sells," so the saying goes. Cosmetics, fashion, and beauty products draw heavily upon sexual themes and physical attraction appealing to the emotion of hope of eternal youth or beauty.

Power

The competitive need to attain status and demonstrate a higher position in the pecking order is another strong motivator. Trigger events that drive purchase behavior often include "keeping up with the Joneses." Prestige products such as designer clothing, Rolex watches, and luxury boats fall into this category; so does membership in exclusive clubs or attendance at highly visible social events. Emotions such as anger, envy, awe, jealousy, competitiveness, pride, and revenge can emerge in this motivation.

Wealth and greed are another facet of power. Triggers can include investment and "get rich quick" schemes that play into these motivations, as do opportunities to start or grow a business, or the desire to climb the corporate ladder if a colleague is promoted. Emotions such as hope, envy, jealousy, anxiety, guilt, fear, and boredom can play a key role in this motivation.

Personal Pursuits

Some people are highly motivated to expand their core of knowledge, lose weight, or exercise through self-improvement. At the extreme, those with narcissistic tendencies also fall into this category. Common emotions in this motivation include hope, empathy, boredom, inquisitiveness, and anxiety.

Providing service to the greater good, such as charity work, often satisfies an internal need through these acts. Devoting efforts to improving conditions or operations for the good of a business also fits in this motivation. Common emotions include compassion, empathy, gratitude, hope, guilt, pity, pride, and happiness.

Of course, we cannot ignore curiosity and fun as powerful drivers of behavior and time. Personal pursuits in the forms of curiosity and self-improvement are often the reason we can spend hours surfing the Internet, losing all track of time. With mysteries, we want to find out what that intriguing headline meant, whodunit, and how it all ends. Fun, of course, is a powerful attractor as well. Common emotions for curiosity and fun motivation are joy, happiness, surprise, suspense, wonder, and desire.

Last but not least, the need for security and safety has a profound effect on personal motivation. Fear and anxiety is a complex motivation relative to time and attention. In some instances, people are triggered to spend time on actions meant to protect their situation, such as pursuing job training after a new management regime takes charge. In other cases—as with fear of a natural disaster such as an earthquake—we can do nothing to prevent the event, so we don't want to spend too much time thinking about it. Instead, we focus a small slice of time and attention on preparation (small because it is unpleasant to think too much about a potential disaster). Products aimed at allaying the fears that fall outside our control often fit better into a convenience, or habit/process perspective, since customers don't have a propensity to sustainably focus time and attention on it. Common emotions include fear, anxiety, annoyance, worry, frustration, and guilt.

Of course, motivations are not mutually exclusive and a person can be driven by several motivations simultaneously. Consider that people could subscribe to a dating website seeking to satisfy their curiosity about who would be their match, to seek social connection, or as a response to physical attraction. From a marketing perspective, identifying the emotional connection points is more important than discerning between them, as humans are complex and may be motivated on several levels, both conscious and unconscious. Determining a trigger strong enough to drive the motivation to the surface of consciousness and action is most important.

Certainly, psychological motivations are not solely the province of the motivation quadrant. However, in the motivation quadrant, psychological motivations are at their most concentrated and sustainable state. When saving money goes beyond basic pragmatism to affect the heart and mind—as when customers pursue "the deal" as a hobby and spend extra time driving from store to store with coupons (and perhaps losing the savings in time spent, gasoline used, and car wear accumulated)—then it is more emotional and motivation driven.

Establishing a Motivation Position

Products that reside in the motivation quadrant garner a high amount of attention and time from the customer. Because of the Time-Value Tradeoff, customers will therefore be sensitive to whether a motivation offering is delivering sufficient value for the time and attention. "Is this worth my time?" will be a common refrain. Providing consistently high value that satisfies an underlying motivation relative to the time invested is a critical element to success in this quadrant.

In chapter 1, I outlined two ways to apply the Time-ographics Framework: evaluate the context by mapping the product and customer activity, and seek opportunities that arise out of potential customer-product combinations. These analyses are a necessary starting point for any company wanting to compete in the motivation quadrant.

From these exercises, innovators and marketers focusing on the motivation quadrant can first identify the sources of motivation involved in the use of their product and the corresponding activities. They should also identify how strong the motivation is likely to be. Is the motivation strong but short-lived, as happens with customers whose interest is piqued by a new fad or a spark of interest? Consider the sandwich spread example we discussed in chapter 1: how sustainably would that appeal to the heart and mind? Is the motivation weak, as it may be with some areas of self-improvement (we know we *should* lose weight, but we don't really want to make the sacrifices to do it)? The strength of motivation is important, because it can help determine whether the offering will address a motivational need at all, or whether it makes sense to start in the motivation quadrant and then move the customer to a more stable quadrant.

Once the context, priorities, and motivations are understood, there are a number of techniques to establish a motivation position. It is impossible to describe them all without writing a compendium of attention-getting marketing and public relations practices. But let's touch here on some of the more contemporary approaches.

Create Mystery

Triggering the curiosity motivation by creating mystery and suspense is one way to tap into a motivation position. Popular television shows like *Lost*, where viewers are kept at the edge of their seat as the plot unfolds, hold attention for long periods of time. Reality shows with contestants that are eliminated, such as *Survivor* and *The Apprentice*, keep viewers coming back to find out who ultimately wins. Yet mystery and curiosity work for more than television shows and movies.

Location-based services using Global Positioning Systems offer unique opportunities to leverage suspense and mystery. Although treasure hunts are not new, the location-based services using GPS offer new opportunities to gain traction with customers. The geocaching phenomenon illustrates the potential of GPS-based motivation plays. According to www.geocaching.com, there are almost a million geocaches worldwide.[3] Geocaches are hidden in nooks and crannies in New York City high-rises and on idyllic creek sides in the Sierra Nevada mountains. Metropolitan New York City holds 389 hidden geocaches. Placed by a community of enthusiasts, these small containers—usually the size of an index card file—are found by "treasure" seekers using GPS devices and the geocaching website. The containers typically hold an entry log and an assortment of trinkets, and the customer is to insert an item and take an item from the container.

The concept of a treasure hunt offers the opportunity for businesses to utilize location-based technology as it becomes more widely adopted and integrated into smartphones. Imagine location-based offers tied to travel guidebooks, with promotional online coupons to local restaurants and attractions inserted in virtual caches and downloaded once the users reach their destination. Smartphone-based scavenger hunt companies like Foursquare, Gowalla, and Wherigo.com have mobile platforms that enable companies to participate in and build their own location-based adventures and promotions.

In Foursquare, for example, users compete for points in their city and vie for the prestigious spot of "mayor" for different locations, all via their smartphones. Businesses that sponsor "mayor specials" offer incentives such as free coffee or ice cream for visiting their store. The thrill of seeking out and "capturing" new locations (curiosity combined with a bit of competitive power motivation for mayorship and badges) makes what could have been a boring mobile advertising application into a mobile scavenger hunt game that is quite addictive for users.

Create a Diagnostic

One way to tap into self-improvement, curiosity, greed, or social-good motivations is through benchmarks. Tools that allow users to answer a set of questions, measure their situation, and then see results are very popular. There are two common ways to develop this approach:

1. Knowledge-based
2. User-contributed or "give to get"

Knowledge-based: These are diagnostics that are built upon knowledge or intellectual property possessed by your firm. Examples include career or personality assessments to identify a person's skills and the corresponding best-fit jobs.

One company that has used knowledge-based diagnostics effectively is HubSpot, a provider of marketing software for small businesses. HubSpot created an online website grader that will evaluate a website for free. This online grading tool measures the marketing effectiveness of your website on a number of criteria, including optimal keywords, and grades your site against your competitors. This diagnostic, having graded more than a million websites and been actively marketed through social media, has driven more than 450,000 leads, of which 2 to 4 percent have converted into HubSpot customers. "We've grown from 300 to 1700 customers in the last twelve months in a down economy," said Dharmesh Shah, CTO and founder of HubSpot.

HubSpot's success with the website diagnostic was achieved not just because it is free, but because the company is very efficient with customer conversion. When a small-business prospect receives their grade, they may want to discuss the results and implications. At the bottom of the report is a clear call to action asking, "Are you disappointed with your grade? Do you need help?" According to Dharmesh, HubSpot maintains a call center where well-trained telesales specialists walk potential customers through the report, including tips for improvement.

User-contributed: "Give to get" diagnostic programs are structured so that the customer submits information, usually through an online survey, into a common database in order to receive a comparison or benchmark result in return. Often the results are a compilation of responses from other respondents in an industry or customer interest group. Glassdoor.com, a salary survey site, collects salary information from employees of major corporations. In return for sharing specific salary information, survey respondents receive comparisons of salaries at major companies such as Bank of America, IBM, and Accenture—a helpful tool when negotiating for better pay or just seeing where you stand in today's environment. Symantec's INFORM program, which I described earlier, is an example of a "give to get" diagnostic because 1,400-plus companies contributed their data to the database and the benchmarks are aggregated based on the inputs.

The advantage of a user-contributed diagnostic is that your company can garner greater industry insight and build intellectual property based on industry or customer data instead of having to develop it on your own. It offers the opportunity to stay on top of the latest trends, because the data and the comparisons are generated from the survey participants. Consider how Symantec utilizes INFORM to help guide future product development decisions based on trends in the data and comments by IT executives. A user-contributed diagnostic is often perceived by buyers as less biased. This is particularly important for product sellers where the customers may be skeptical of the findings if they believe a knowledge-based diagnostic is slanted in favor of the company's products or services.

User-contributed diagnostics also derive competitive advantage and traction through greater customer participation. The more customers that complete the survey, the stronger the benchmark becomes. A user-contributed benchmark is typically more difficult to replicate. From a

Time-Value Tradeoff perspective, customers will be drawn to participate in benchmarks that provide the broadest base of opinion representing their industry or segment. However, gaining a sufficient number of responses in a user-contributed diagnostic at the beginning can be tricky, because customers are being asked to participate with a lower-value return—it usually requires incentives and special promotion to get off the ground.

Keep in mind that long-term traction can be attained from diagnostics only if the results are dynamic, robust, and drive action credibly. Consider the difference between the Symantec INFORM program and the latest social network pop poll.

Make Your Customer the Star

Another way to establish a motivation quadrant position is to personalize an offering for the customer and make that customer the center of the products. Cosmetic sites such as Mary Kay offer virtual makeovers for participants. Users can upload a photo and experiment with colors and trendy looks in the comfort of their home, without traveling to a busy department store. Such sites enable users to customize and select their favorite looks. The site automatically generates a shopping cart for online checkout with a local dealer.

In the future, options will exist to further integrate customer images directly into offerings such as movies, learning, stories, and games through virtual reality and simulation technology. Companies such as BigStage, VirtualHeroes, and PrimeSense enable the capture of 3D images of the customer and realistic interactive simulation.

Become the Destination

Another way to establish a motivation position is to allow customers to linger and create dwell time spaces. Although we all have limited time, we also want destinations that delight us and provide a superior customer experience. Two notable examples, Starbucks and Panera Bread, not only provide food, they also offer a comfortable atmosphere.[4] Rather than rushing people out the door to free up table space, Panera encourages customers to hang out with free Wi-Fi service.

In e-commerce, "magalogs" (a combination of magazines and catalogs) are becoming more common. A magalog integrates the interest-generating elements of a magazine with an e-commerce store. To illustrate, *Lucky* magazine's website provides the ultimate destination for fashionistas, combining the latest trends with lists of items that celebrities buy and even offering an easy-click shopping cart. Similar magalogs have emerged that target gourmet cooks and other segments.

Social Shopping

I would be remiss for not mentioning social media as a tool for creating social attraction and for establishing a position in the motivation quadrant.

We like to share new things with our friends but can't always get together with them. Facebook Connect is a small application (widget) that is inserted onto an e-commerce site that allows consumers to send links of items they are interested in buying to select Facebook friends for their opinion. As of late 2009, 43 percent of online retailers have reportedly signed up, with an additional 31 percent planning to join in 2010.[5] Although it is too early to tell whether social shopping will be broadly accepted by the marketplace, it taps into important peer and power motivations.

Create a Halo Effect

Cause marketing, in which a product associates itself with a charity or humanitarian sector, has built significant momentum in the past decade, as marketers marry the purchaser's impulse to do good with traditional marketing. German auto manufacturer Volkswagen seems to be embracing social causes through its Fun Theory (www.the funtheory.com) contest. The Fun Theory encourages contestants to come up with ideas that motivate people to take actions that are good for them or for the planet while tapping into fun and social-good motivations. Volkswagen produced viral YouTube videos that highlight several concepts, including a glass recycling container that lets the recycler accrue points as in an arcade game, and a "staircase piano" that plays music when a person walks on it, encouraging people to take the stairs instead of the escalator. Though Volkswagen's sponsorship is clear, the connection between the social ideas and the automotive business is indirect, but may ultimately enhance their image because viewers are not turned off by "in your face" advertising—thus creating a halo effect.[6]

According to industry sources, 72 percent of customers have purchased a particular brand because they knew that the brand supported a cause they believed in.[7] Also, 85 percent have a more positive image of a company that supports a cause they care about, and 79 percent are likely to switch from one brand to another (price and quality equal) if the other brand is associated with a good cause.[8]

Sustaining a Motivation Position

Okay, so you've got their time and attention. Now what? While it is challenging to establish a motivation position, sustaining such a position has its own distinct difficulties. Competing forces vie for time and attention and erode an offering's position. Nothing lasts forever, and time-and-attention entropy takes hold. For this reason, this quadrant is not for the timid. Because of the precarious nature of the motivation position, constant investment in the position is essential.

Organizational competencies. Companies like Apple and Disney tend to fare well in this quadrant. A key reason is that they have internal operational processes, employee skills, and knowledge to manage a continual flow of innovation that sustains and renews the attention of their customers. Winners in this quadrant are cognizant that their product will hold a position with the customer for a finite period of time, and they actively manage product life cycles in line with this attention process. Key attributes of an organization tuned to sustain a motivation quadrant position include creativity, trend-spotting, organizational adaptability, and the ability to embrace, communicate, and promote new ideas.

These organizations are keenly aware of the emotional and motivational triggers that drive action. Many of the activities associated with traditional marketing and branding are present in this quadrant, in addition to the capability to develop and launch new products rapidly. Because of constant attention and time erosion, managing product life cycles (both introduction and end of life) are important. Increasingly, the ability to have two-way engagement through the use of Web 2.0 technologies plays into this space, as customers want to take time to have conversations about your product or the activity associated with it. Blogs, social networks, and their ilk are good tools for this quadrant. Let's explore several specific ways companies can sustain a motivation quadrant position in more detail. (Tables 3–1 and 3–2 highlight some examples.)

Increase your share of customer time. There is a common adage among parents of teenagers: "To keep your kids out of trouble, keep

Motivation Quadrant: Market Traction Examples (I)

Time-Value Elements / Options	TIME-OGRAPHICS CONTEXT	TIME BOUNDARY STRATEGIES	TECHNOLOGY ENABLERS	MARKET TRACTION
Increase Share of Customer Time *e.g., Kindle*	• Personal Pursuits • Self-improvement Hold interest • Fun/Curiosity	• Dwell time • Increase Time–Value • Integrate purchasing with consumption	• Auto link to e-commerce (Kindle) • Mobile/Web technology	• Time window dominance • Inertia • Time-relevant value
Keep It Fresh *e.g., Digital Chocolate*	• Personal Pursuits: curiosity/fun • Peers: social • Hold interest–what's new	• Time slicing "Seize the Minute!" • Link to future time windows NanoStars™	• Mobile • Rapid innovation platform • Cross-platform	• Time-relevant value • Seeking • Virtual characters cross-games
Diagnostic/ Track Trends *e.g., Nike+ HubSpot*	• Personal Pursuits: Track improvement, Curiosity	• Increase time-value through industry benchmarks, trend data • Link to future time window	• Wireless shoe sensor data collection & monitoring • Trend graphs & analytics	• Inertia: Data personalized, baseline data • Time-relevant value

Table 3–1: Options to sustain traction with motivation products (Part I)

them busy." The same holds true for customers: companies holding a motivation quadrant position should keep customers engaged—distracted, even—with their offerings to prevent them from spending time with competitors. As we saw with the Webkinz story described previously, keeping customers busy can create a competitive advantage. Examples of effective time-blocking techniques are websites or retail stores that increase dwell time through cross-selling or customer education.

This works best when customers are engaged, even entertained, so they don't know they are spending so much time. Disney does this very well at their theme parks; anyone who has ever visited Disney World knows that between the number of rides and concessions and the size of the resort, visitors can vacation an entire week without giving money to anyone other than the Disney Corporation. Customers have only a few weeks a year of vacation. Every day and dollar Disney captures is lost forever by competitors. If your company doesn't have the vast resources of Disney, you can increase your share of customer time through alliances and affiliate relationships with complementary partners.

Build a rapid innovation platform. Another way to hold customer interest over time is by "keeping it fresh." This can be accomplished either by innovating a steady stream of new products or add-ons that incorporate new designs or new functions, or by introducing new content or ideas to promote thought leadership. Fashion—a sector where keeping it fresh is the name of the game—highlights the challenge of pressing this strategic lever for motivation. The expectation of seasonal renewal puts products leaning on the "keep it fresh" lever in a constant battle for customer time. Only the best market visionaries with trend-catching competencies can sustain this for a long period of time without the aid of technology or business methods to create stickiness.

One way to keep pace with trends in a sustainable way is to create a common technology platform. Digital Chocolate, highlighted in chapter 2, designed its operational platform to enable rapid development and distribution of new products. According to founder Trip Hawkins, most game providers license content from third parties and then distribute the games to the market, much the way Hollywood distributors buy distribution rights to films made by someone else. A part of bringing the games to market involves reworking them to operate on multiple mobile platforms. Digital Chocolate addressed this challenge by creating a standard technology base.

The technology platform enables Digital Chocolate partners to develop games more quickly. Trip reports that this facilitates rapid integration and distribution of new games on multiple mobile platforms including the iPhone. As the popularity of a particular game wanes, Digital Chocolate is able to launch new games rapidly to keep customers engaged and interested. "With our integrated technology base, we are able to introduce more than 30 new games or sequels a year," adds Trip.

Track trend data over time. Customers find it useful to understand how information pertaining to their experience trends over time. As we saw, Nike keeps customers returning willingly to their site by tracking performance with the Nike+ sensors, which update the site after a run. Diet websites such as Weight Watchers provide similar tools that allow visitors to track their progress to a goal. Data-based tools create the opportunity to build an emotional relationship with customers, and offer add-on products such as additional running gear, training information, or packaged foods.

Trend data can also decrease customer turnover, since the sponsor is the only one that holds the baseline data and the data points. With Nike+ and other diagnostics, the data cannot be easily copied and moved to a competitor, and because of Time-Value Tradeoffs, the customer is less willing to spend time duplicating efforts with a competitor for similar results.

Share knowledge over an activity life cycle. Motivated customers tend to seek knowledge. Consider expectant mothers that are excited about the changes taking place in the fetus's development, and in their own bodies. Procter & Gamble, the makers of Pampers, have recognized this broader motivation and introduced widgets or information feeds for expectant mothers.[9] Pampers' Village Pregnancy widget delivers a personalized countdown clock to delivery and provides weekly updates on what is happening during each period of the pregnancy.[10] The widget also connects directly to the Pampers Village website, which contains resources and information on the stages of pregnancy, as well as on children's early development, from infanthood through preschool.[11] This content creates a motivation for customers to return repeatedly to the website. It also enables P&G to build a relationship with the customer. By understanding the exact delivery date, P&G is able to identify when diaper products are needed, as well as other baby-related products. The company has even developed a mobile capacity to allow for notifications via SMS. This resource plays on motivations such as curiosity ("How has my baby grown this week?") and family ("Am I doing all the right things for my baby?).

Keep customers in suspense. As we saw earlier, mystery and suspense can trigger the curiosity motivation and can keep customers coming back.

Mysteries and treasure hunts are not limited to promotions. Products can offer elements of this as well. Imagine a training program, novel, mobile movie, or exercise program whose story unfolds as the "reader" moves through the real world. These could also allow users to select their own adventure, where the outcome changes dependent on

Motivation Quadrant: Market Traction Examples (II)

Time-Value Elements / Options	TIME-OGRAPHICS CONTEXT	TIME BOUNDARY STRATEGIES	TECHNOLOGY ENABLERS	MARKET TRACTION
Become a Knowledge Source e.g., *Pampers Widget*	• Personal Pursuits: Curiosity Self-improvement • Fastest knowledge source	• Low time commitment • Time-critical value • Time slicing info over 9+ months	• Widgets • Reminders & updates • Resident on desktop	• Inertia: Easy info access and familiarity • Time-relevant value
Keep Them in Suspense e.g., *GPS Treasure Hunt*	• Personal Pursuits: Curiosity/Fun–What will happen next?	• Increase Time-Value • Dwell time	• Location-based & virtual treasure hunt applications	• Inertia: Owning the story and the reveal • Seeking
Avoid Loss of Status e.g., *Season Ticket Seats*	• Peers: Fun/Social • Power: Fear of loss • Learning curve or earned status	• Link to future time window	• Database tracking earned status	• Inertia: More benefits to stay (*carrot*)
Create Social Glue e.g., *Private Social Network*	• Peers: Social • Power: Status	• Increase Time-Value: Social, right people	• Community software	• Time-relevant value: Network effects

Table 3–2: Options to sustain traction with motivation offerings (Part II)

the path the reader takes. Proactively managing the product life cycle by introducing new motivation products when the end of the mystery is revealed can sustain the customer's attention.

Avoid loss of status. Venues and services with limited but differentiated classes, such as professional sports teams and airlines, have been particularly adept at developing programs where participants earn the ability to be placed in a certain class or status. This is an example of linking to future time windows. Consider that season ticket holders must buy season tickets every year to keep the best seats. Continue to buy and you may be moved to a better seat—a nice carrot to keep you buying. Miss a year? You go back to the nosebleed seats. This is also true for certain summer camps, where people sign up every year to hold their preferred week and accommodations—or else there may not be a space for them to return the following year. This technique plays into the deep motivations of status, fear, and security, as well as social/camaraderie if family and friends are involved.

Create social glue. Another way to sustain a motivation position is to enable customers who share similar motivations and interests to spend useful time together.

Professional online communities allow businesspeople to congregate and discuss common interests and best practices. Such communities exist for teachers, tax consultants, marketing officers, database administrators, or any other profession that could benefit from a community of peers. A number of motivations are at work in these communities, including the desire for self-improvement by learning from others, and the desire for status through association with people who may advance your career, or even curiosity, as community members return to see what's new.

With the network effect, once connections have been established and content has been loaded, it is difficult to ask a network of colleagues to defect as well. Moving to an alternative requires being willing to sacrifice not just time in recreating one's profile, but a great deal of the value of the network, since the new network will be smaller than the old one. The risk of being seen as a social outcast plays into motivations here.

Why Motivation Offerings Fail to Hold Their Position

Many businesses strive to create a connection with the heart or mind of the customer, yet even the best companies don't win every time. Customers are fickle, and their needs and interests change quickly. But just as often, the seller gets the Time-Value wrong. Here are some frequent reasons why motivation offerings fail:

Poor timing. Similar to thinking about the right time to ask a boss for a raise, or your spouse for a favor, you must consider that customers have different levels of receptivity to a motivation offering at different times. Many people are not open to talking about business ideas while on vacation, and when people use Facebook they are significantly less inclined to click through on ads than they would be on other websites. According to Tom Bedecarre, chief executive of independent digital-ad firm AKQA, advertising doesn't fit so neatly into a conversation that people are having among themselves. He indicates that the interruptive model of advertising hasn't been successful.[12]

In addition to personal timing, market timing can cause motivation offerings to fail, as two pioneering social media sites, Six Degrees and SocialNet, found out when they were introduced in the late 1990s. "We all basically hit the market several years before the market was ready for social networking," said Reid G. Hoffman, founding chief executive of SocialNet and an early investor in Friendster.[13] Similarly, technology delays can cause offerings to miss a market window while newer technology displaces it. By the time the technology of two-way pagers had matured to a point of commercial viability, small cell phones with "push to talk" features were available and displaced them.

Poor linkage between the motivation and the product. While there are products that unquestionably belong in the value, convenience, or habit quadrants for most users, these same product types may be motivational for a subset of customers. Consider that the vast majority of homes do just fine with a generic set of commodity kitchen knives. But gourmet home chefs will be motivated to buy an expensive, fine set of knives because it is important to the quality of their results in the kitchen. The question for companies that view their product as motivational *for some* is whether it is motivational *for enough*. There are two potential traps for companies in this situation.

The first trap is overestimating the number of customers that are motivated. Washington Mutual (WaMu), the bank that found itself at the epicenter of the sub-prime lending debacle, at one time was known for the personal touch it took with customers. Years ago the bank placed a bet on the fact that there was a sizeable segment of customers that wanted warm-and-fuzzy retail branches where they could sit down and have a face-to-face with a banking agent. They invested more than $1 billion to replace traditional bank teller windows and bulletproof glass with futuristic freestanding counters with designer touches.[14] Yet this motivation-driven strategy never seemed to differentiate WaMu in most of the markets it penetrated. In the Chicago area, according to the Federal Deposit Insurance Corporation, WaMu held just 0.6 percent of all deposits as of June 30, 2008, placing it 25th among all banks and savings institutions.[15]

Overestimating the size of a motivated market is something almost any product or service may be vulnerable to, since there are always going to be groups of people highly devoted to even the most esoteric or seemingly trivial products. The challenge for executives is to size the opportunity in each quadrant that applies and determine whether a large enough niche exists to pursue a motivation opportunity. This can be more difficult than it sounds, because the small group of motivated customers will always dominate feedback channels. Those outside the motivation quadrant won't take the time to fill out surveys, send emails, call comment lines, or register for newsletters. This is an even bigger issue today, with the adoption of social media. Your marketing department may be listening to a vocal minority with little spending power, when a quiet majority with considerable financial resources wants something entirely different.

Fads. Our society craves what is new and different. The seasonal shifts toward the next thing often result in fads that reveal themselves as ridiculous mere seconds after purchase. How can you distinguish between a fad and a trend? Perhaps one of the best ways is to determine whether the product has the respect of the customer and is not a theme for college parties or comedies. Consider Slankets, form-fitting blankets with sleeves and a thick Franciscan-like collar. Initially designed for Midwestern seniors to curl up on a couch with a magazine and turn pages without pulling their arms from under the blanket, Slankets became popular cult attire for college festivities and evenings on the town. In contrast, environmental awareness or "green" is a trend, because most purchasers take it seriously. Although it will go through its cycle, as we saw a green trend during the 1970s, it will last longer than a few seasons of college toga parties.

Limited life offerings. A product does not have to be a fad to be vulnerable to natural obsolescence brought about by the product life cycle. New versions of products or product categories improve on the old, encouraging replacement. In 2005, the Motorola RAZR was the "gotta have it" cell phone. But RAZR was quickly overtaken by the iPhone and other smartphones.[16] Any marketer that is going to rely on "cool" features for its motivation must be willing to invest every year to keep ahead of the curve.

Transitioning Quadrants

This chapter has identified ways to establish or maintain a motivational position, and has identified the causes of many motivational failures. Companies need not assume, however, that their products must adhere to a "once motivational, always motivational" strategy. Because motivational offerings are associated with such strong emotions, logic predicts that customers grow very attached and loyal to them, but in fact the opposite is true. The high amount of time and attention required to maintain a top-of-mind position with the customer is very difficult to sustain. Rather than continually pounding consumers with attention-getting tactics aimed at keeping the product in the motivation position, companies can grab attention in the motivation quadrant, then transition the customer to a more sustainable quadrant. For example, over time, as customers repeat an activity, or turn the activity into a default action through automatic payments or renewals, motivations may evolve into habits. Although HubSpot uses a motivation-based diagnostic, the product itself is a subscription-based software product that automatically renews every month. "We had about 350 percent growth in sales over the past twelve months, projected to another 300 percent in the next twelve months. It's like clockwork; it's a subscription, so the revenue growth is very predictable to us," states Dharmesh Shah, founder and CTO of HubSpot.

Let's turn to the habit quadrant in the next chapter to understand how to develop and maintain a position when customers are on autopilot.

CHAPTER 3: TWO-MINUTE TAKEAWAYS

Products that reside in the motivation quadrant demand the highest amount of time and attention from consumers because they connect to things people really care about: Peers (family and friends), Power (status and greed), and Personal Pursuits (self-improvement, curiosity, fun, fear). Many companies aspire to motivation status, but seller beware—it is difficult to establish a motivation position and difficult to sustain one because of constant distraction.

A few of the new rules that apply to establishing or maintaining a motivation position:

- *Rule:* Capture opportunities that emerge from multitasking and distraction.
- *Tool:* Leverage the multitasking instinct to seek information.
- *Rule:* Differentiate on customer time priorities.
- *Tool:* Enable customers to fulfill motivations in new contexts to open up new segments of nonconsumers.
- *Rule:* View customers as situational.
- *Tool:* Launch motivation products only when and where motivations are triggered and customers can pay attention.
- *Rule:* Grow by shifting time boundaries.
- *Tool:* Help customers fulfill motivations through dwell time to crowd out competing offerings.
- *Rule:* Focus on customer time to evaluate, purchase, and consume.
- *Tool:* Motivation offerings will be constantly under attack as other activities vie for attention—innovate to keep consumers interested and occupied.
- *Rule:* Create advantage through customer inertia and time-relevant value.
- *Tool:* Develop customized products with customer data and attributes that resonate with motivations.

4

TIME ON AUTOPILOT: HABIT QUADRANT PRODUCTS

■

"We are what we repeatedly do."
<small>ARISTOTLE</small>

My friend Tim works from home. His office is on the first floor, and his bedroom is on the second. Recently he was telling me how often he finds himself "accidentally" brushing his teeth in the middle of the day. As Tim says, "I'll be working on a project, thinking about some data point that I want to use, when I realize that I left the book in the study upstairs. So I go to get it—and a few minutes later I find myself standing in front of the mirror in the bathroom, brushing my teeth. The last thing I really remember is starting up the stairs." Somewhere on the stairs, while he's deep in thought, Tim's autopilot kicks in and takes over.

It's hard to admit how many things each of us do by habit. In fact, our habits, our internal autopilot, are so strong that it's hard to notice how much we do without even thinking about it. When I informally quiz people about how much of their daily activity is unconscious, most guess an average of 10 percent. Psychological studies estimate that the real figure for repetitive and unthinking behavior is about 45 percent.[1] According to research psychologist Dr. Aric Sigman, "We all subconsciously employ habit or routine—whether we are time poor or not."[2] As much as we'd like to believe that we're exercising judgment and thoughtful consideration, constant distraction and our limited attention spans force us, like Tim, to turn on the autopilot for a considerable part of each day.

Challenging Wired Habits: Bing versus Google

To demonstrate how habits create competitive advantage, consider Google's search engine. When Google started in Susan Wojcicki's Silicon Valley garage in 1998, it was late to the search game already underway between a number of well-funded, well-known incumbents. Despite the odds, Google managed to differentiate itself and capture the attention of Web users with what was, for the time, a superior search experience. Whether or not Google's engine remains superior is now beside the point; today, most users automatically turn to Google out of habit. In fact, a little over 65 percent of U.S. Internet searches are conducted with Google, and users dedicate an average of 11.3 minutes per day, with Google racking up billions of Google website hits per month.[3] This may not sound like much time, especially when we consider that Google is consumed in bite-sized Internet searches throughout the day. However, compare Google's per-day total of 11.3 minutes to the six minutes or so that U.S. consumers devote daily to the universe of online commerce sites and Google's dominance is clear.

Traditional strategy suggests that Google holds little strategic advantage. Its services are not unique, its competitors are not obscure, and its customers are not captive. Alternative search engines such as Microsoft's Bing, Ask, and Yahoo! are well known and easily accessed. Yet Google continues to command the lion's share of the search engine market, more than all other major competitors combined.[4]

As Google's large market share demonstrates, habits can create sustainable competitive advantage and, once established, can be parlayed into particularly lucrative businesses. This has paid off handsomely for Google, as reflected in its $8 billion cash-flow run rate.[5]

Undoubtedly, other companies would like a share of the search market. In 2009, Microsoft challenged Google's market dominance through the introduction of Bing.[6] Bing had a reported advertising budget of $90 million,[7] large enough that Steve Ballmer, Microsoft's CEO, had to personally sign off on it. "When I approved the budget, I gulped, and a gulp in a $60 billion company, well, that's a big gulp," he said.[8] According to reports, Ballmer is willing to invest 5 to 10 percent of Microsoft's operating budget over a five-year period to gain share in the search business.[9]

Two years earlier, Ask.com launched a similar effort by transforming AskJeeves into Ask.com. The company reportedly spent $57 million in 2007 and 2008 on the rebranding campaign, with little to show for it. Then in 2009, the company brought its virtual mascot Jeeves out of retirement, gave him a makeover to update his appearance, and introduced him back into the U.K. market. As these efforts demonstrate, displacing a competitor in a habit position is hard work.

Microsoft developed a motivation-driven, splashy brand advertising campaign and made fundamental changes to the search engine capabilities. For example, Microsoft incorporated a cash-back feature into the shopping functionality. Similar to cash-back referral services such as Ebates.com, Bing pays cash back to users for purchases searched and bought through their engine. In this case, if a user clicks through the Bing site to a commerce site, the user will receive a cash-back rebate if more than $5 in savings is accrued in his or her Bing shopping account.

As of the date of this writing, these capabilities have had minimal impact on Google's share. As one Millennial told me, "I use Bing for product purchases and Google for the rest of my searches." When I asked him, "Why don't you use Bing for all of your searches?" he responded, "I don't know why. Google is just a habit." Whether the additional Bing benefits are sufficient to break the Google addiction is yet unknown. As of February 2010, Bing's share has increased in the U.S. search market; however, it appears to have made its gains from companies such as Yahoo!, Comcast, and others, while Google's share held steady at around 65 percent.[10]

What does this mean for you? It may be a wake-up call to try to pay a bit more attention to the daily routines of your customers. More so, it should alert you to the possibility that what may seem to be low barriers to entry (such as simply typing in a URL) in a traditional strategy analysis may actually be a competitive fortress after all. An analysis of Time-Value Tradeoffs and an understanding of the habit quadrant explain customer behavior in this area.

Brain and Background Processes Drive Routines

Products that reside in the habit quadrant are characterized in two ways:

1. **Brain habits:** This is traditionally what we think of when we say "habits." These are the kinds of habits that are embedded unconsciously into our behavior, and we usually are not aware of them. Brain habits, such as using Google, are often unintentional. The screen is up and we are off and running before we even recognize that we initiated a search. As you will discover in this chapter, Google holds many key attributes of successful habit-driven offerings.
2. **Background processes:** These are products in our lives or our businesses to which we proactively choose to minimize attention. Although important, we prefer to keep these at a low level of consciousness so we are able to pay more attention to other areas of our lives. Computer "brains" in the background typically run these repetitive processes while we attend to daily activities. Sometimes this is accomplished through human outsourcing. Ultimately these processes can be best described as "set it and forget it," as customers do not want to consciously think about them any more than needed. Insurance, bank accounts, and certain software programs for home or business fall into this category.

To keep things simple, when I refer to the "habit quadrant" it will include both brain habits and background processes unless specified otherwise. Although it involves little conscious attention, the habit quadrant accounts for a significant amount of customer activity and behavior. If your market positioning and go-to-market strategies don't take habits and routines into account, you'll waste a lot of money marketing and selling to convince customers to switch to your offering and wonder why it is not working. The opportunity with the habit quadrant is not to focus on how customers make conscious choices as we would expect to see in the convenience and motivation quadrants, but to explore the ways you can enable distracted customers to make automatic choices in your favor.

Brain Habits—Predicting Where Jane Will Go Next

Recent research suggests that human behavior patterns are not only repetitive, but also very predictable. Professor Alex (Sandy) Pentland and his team at the MIT Media Lab conducted research on the schedules and behavior patterns of students, researchers, and executives at MIT. The research team outfitted more than 100 individuals with custom-designed mobile electronic tracking devices (a.k.a. "black boxes") that stayed with the subjects as they traveled around the Boston area. These devices monitored their subjects continuously, whether they were eating, sleeping, traveling to and from work, going to meetings, or socializing. The black boxes monitored subtle details about where the individuals traveled, how quickly they traveled, their body language, and tone of voice.[11]

This experiment revealed that a good 90 percent of what most people do in any day follows such entrenched routines that behavior can be predicted with just a few mathematical equations.[12] Researchers could predict if a subject was headed to the store or to a friend's apartment. Pentland suggests that we like to think of ourselves as free-willed, conscious beings, yet watch people closely and you will find that we are more instinctual and a lot more like other creatures than we care to think.[13]

Our routines and habits aren't just affecting our tooth brushing or daily commute. They also immediately translate to commerce. As we've seen, studies have shown that grocery shoppers tend to fall into a pattern of buying mostly the same items every week. Stress has also been shown to make the habit formation centers of the brain thrive while the conscious decision-making and goal-directed behaviors shrivel.[14] And we all know the level of stress most people are under these days.

Habits and Brand Loyalty

There is a huge difference between brand loyalty, which is a genuine factor in the motivation quadrant, and habits. Real brand loyalty is in play when customers take the time and attention to think about competing brands and choose the one they prefer. In habit buying, on the other hand, customers give minimal attention to the purchase; they are not reflecting on product features or brand promise and deciding to stick with one product over another. They don't want to think about it. They are simply picking up the same orange bottle of detergent that they pick up every time.

What is difficult to discern is how intrinsically attached those customers are to the brand when they awaken from their habit. Some customers will not remember brand attachments, while others will realize that new competitive options are available. Those customers will be the ones vulnerable to defection.

Others may harbor deep-seated loyalty that may have been the reason for placing this product in the habit quadrant in the first place, such as "My mother always used Tide." The key issue for executives is that this is difficult to know, and it is difficult to discern true intentions just by asking. Consumers are acting out of habit, even though they don't know it, and will not often know the real reasons if you ask them.

More important questions go deeper and relate to why they continue to buy a particular product through the lens of Time-Value, triggers, financial switching costs, and emotional ties that entangle them to that status quo purchase. Once we understand those considerations, we can determine what it will take to acquire the customer. The customer may like cavity protection and think highly of your brand, but if it doesn't exceed her threshold for Time-Value and if there is no trigger to prompt change, there is no conversion to sales. *Nada.*

Why We Don't Want to Think About Some Products We Buy

Have you ever gotten a call from an insurance agent, bank, or software sales representative and said, "Now is not a good time"? For many background processes, customers purposefully take up-front time to set up such services to their liking (such as a bank account that links automatic deposits), so they don't have to bother devoting more attention to it later. The goal of background processes is to purposefully reduce attention. The customer just wants to know it works. There is a conscious decision to be less conscious.[15]

If your customer's goal is to purposefully reduce the attention devoted to your product because she doesn't want to think about it, you definitely have the elements of a background process offering—we don't tend to think of our Internet service providers, insurance providers, security services, software utilities, and banks as convenience products. Although these are important, most people would like to focus their limited attention elsewhere.

Status quo bias—a term used by behavioral psychologists and economists that describes the tendency for people to be risk averse and avoid change—plays a big role in background processes. People certainly don't want to go through the process of evaluation and setup of a new product again if they can avoid it. They've got too many other activities on their agenda.

Triggers and the Prairie Dog Effect

According to B. J. Fogg of Stanford University, willingness and ability are not sufficient conditions to prompt behavior change. A trigger must be involved to prompt action.[16] What I have also learned through my work is that not all triggers are equal. The strength of triggers can vary, and a stronger trigger is needed to prompt someone in the habit quadrant to switch to a competitive offering. We may be discontent with the services provided by our current telecom service, payroll provider, or bank, but is the Time-Value significant enough to justify the time to evaluate and transition to a new provider? And when we are satisfied, we have very little incentive to switch, since other items in our lives take priority. As we have seen, these services are important, but not the types of activities most of us enjoy devoting attention to in our business or personal lives.

Without a trigger, consumers and executives get annoyed when competitors attempt to call on them. They may actually defend their current solution, not from a position of product loyalty, but from a position of protecting their time and attention. They don't want to think about it, and this salesperson is forcing them to pay attention to it.

This is a powerful force that can work in your favor if customers are kept satisfied. Consider the competitive implications of this for a moment: by working with the forces of time and attention, your customers will repel the competition on your behalf. They don't have to emotionally love your brand; however, the customers in this quadrant need to be satisfied with your product so that they don't want to pursue the effort to switch.

Yet if your bank made a financial error, or your software stopped working, you would be immediately triggered to look at alternatives. I call this phenomenon the Prairie Dog Effect because the behavior described is reminiscent of prairie dogs, animals native to the U.S. Midwestern plains that are best known for peeking out of their holes and looking around.

When customers reside in the habit quadrant they often behave in much the same way. The job of a company in this quadrant is to keep existing customers comfortable and happy in their "burrow" so they have little reason to "prairie dog" by popping their heads up from their comfortable existence to look at competing alternatives. Looking around involves a higher level of awareness, but it is short-lived, because the customers have a desire to fix the problem quickly so they can devote attention to other priorities. Although this involves a burst of attention, the product is still considered a habit quadrant product at heart because the overall propensity to devote attention is low. The Prairie Dog Effect is a key attribute of customer behavior in this quadrant and informs key actions to pursue under the new rules.

If you are seeking to acquire new customers that reside in the habit quadrant of your competitors, then you need to identify and watch for Prairie Dog events. It is at these trigger points that your competitors are most vulnerable to defection, because customers are consciously seeking alternatives and will pay attention to your contact.

The Value of Habits

The idea of living in the habit quadrant may seem uncomfortable to many. If a customer is using a product out of habit, then there seems to be no place for the control and influence that product developers, marketers, and even executives try to exert. A company or product success becomes solely dependent on the unconscious actions of consumers.

Many have a reflexive distaste for living in the habit quadrant because, well, habit doesn't seem very "sexy." It's not where the action is, which makes marketers struggle to develop that next splashy advertising campaign that will assure everyone in the organization that "marketing is adding value" and ensure that the chief marketing officer's (CMO) tenure will last longer than the usual 26.8 months.[17]

Of course, for CEOs there's nothing sexier than profitability. And although Google doesn't advertise much in the traditional sense, the company is certainly well regarded in the market. Companies that succeed in creating habits receive a significant boost to their top and bottom lines. On the top line, habit generates consistent and steady revenue. On the bottom line, we've all heard the familiar statistic that it can cost five times as much to acquire a new customer as to keep an existing one.[18]

As I'll explain, an executive with a successful habit-based product seeks primarily to make sure that everything is running smoothly, quietly adds value that further deepens the relationship, increases the average selling price, and ensures the customer never needs to devote attention to the purchase. And far from being dull or unchallenging, the creation and maintenance of habits requires a much savvier and systematic approach to product development and marketing than the traditional approach of constantly introducing new products and making noise in the market. Customer habits are hard to make and even harder to break. This is a powerful competitive position.

Establishing a Habit Quadrant Position

How do you create a habit? To get to this state requires building the mental or system patterns that enable autopilot to take over and attention to shift elsewhere. We can do so by satisfying three prerequisites for brain habits: a cue, high frequency, and fast feedback. Once we have the prerequisites, we can then identify ways to insert these habits into people's routines, and prepare your company to have an unfettered path to ensure customer adoption. Let's step through these in more detail by starting with the prerequisites.

Cue: A cue is a remarkably powerful environmental input—such as Pavlov's bell, or the bell that dings in your car to fasten your seat belt—that helps invoke a learned response or behavior pattern. For example, the mere sight of food stimulates us to eat, and one study showed that office workers ate 3.1 more chocolate candies when the candy was placed on the desk in clear jars than when the candy was placed in opaque jars.[19] Cues also explain why it's so difficult to stick to a diet. We all have eating habits that have been deeply ingrained via high frequency and fast feedback—and those habits are tied to environmental cues around our house and workplace. Research on automatic behaviors suggests that rather than focusing on what to eat or not to eat (which involves the conscious portions of the brain), shaping the food environment (such as not keeping cookies in the house) generates better results for dieters.[20]

High frequency: It is very difficult to create a new habit with an activity or product that is not used regularly because the mental pattern-building that underlies habits happens only via repetition. The more time that elapses between repetitions, the less likely the mental pattern is going to be formed. High frequency can take the form of either frequent purchases or frequent use.

Fast feedback: A third crucial part of building mental patterns is that the user gets fast, usually positive, feedback from engaging in the habit. There are lots of ways to deliver this feedback, which I'll explore a little later in this chapter, but more important than how the feedback is delivered is the speed. The user needs to be able to unequivocally connect cause and positive effect for maximum habit-forming potential. Studies have shown that positive encouragement, even from a computer, has a favorable effect on how people feel about themselves and the capability of the computer program—even when fully aware that the feedback is computer generated.[21] In employee and customer interactions alike, carrots are always better than sticks.

A great example of a habit-forming product/service we can all (often somewhat sheepishly) relate to is the BlackBerry. Not only does a user receive a buzz (the cue) with the arrival of each new message (high frequency), but once you pick it up you see the new message immediately and can fire off a response quickly, which gives the fast feedback of feeling like you've accomplished something. Have you ever noticed people in an infinite loop constantly checking their BlackBerry even when it's not buzzing? This is an outcome of a habit.

Technology is definitely an ally in meeting these three primary criteria of the habit quadrant. Technology allows many more applications delivered on platforms like the BlackBerry and iPhone to move from low to high frequency. The broader deployment of mobile technologies, always-on sensors, and GPS chips means that more products and services can become habits than ever before.

With aging populations, and the high cost of healthcare, new mobile health and wellness offerings are emerging that help individuals to develop healthy habits on their own. One company capitalizing on this mobile trend is Silicon Valley virtual health-coaching startup Vive (www.vivecoach.com). Vive allows users to set a few simple health goals such as eating right, exercising, or taking prescription medication and sends a text reminder at a pre-set time to the user's phone to cue the person to perform the desired habit. The user responds to the text about whether the goal was met and can jot notes about progress. The website program automatically charts daily progress against the goal and sends encouragement and tips to the user. The goal of Vive's service is to become a trusted virtual health coach that empowers and helps users to follow through on daily health activities.[22]

So if you have a product that has elements that lend themselves to a habit, how do you actually create one?[23]

HOW MANY REPETITIONS DOES IT TAKE TO FORM A HABIT?

Although we know that frequency is important, a question that arises is how many times an activity needs to be repeated to form a brain habit. An often mis-cited statistic is that it takes 21 days to form a habit. There is little evidence for this, as it appears to have come from a book written in 1960 by a physician who noticed that amputees took, on average, 21 days to stop reflexively attempting to use their missing limb.[24] I certainly hope that your customers don't need to lose a limb in order to figure out how to use your products. Recent research appears more relevant and pragmatic—the number of repetitions depends on the difficulty of the change for the individual.

Researchers at the University College, London, recruited 96 people who were interested in forming a new habit ranging from drinking a glass of water daily to performing 50 sit-ups every day. What they found was that simply to adopt tasks such as drinking a glass of water took only 18 days of repetition, but more difficult tasks such as performing sit-ups or running took as much as 254 days to form habit. The study revealed a 66-day mean to form the behaviors in the test.[25]

Tapping into Routines—
Why Hand-Sanitizer Dispensers Are Everywhere

One way to develop a habit is to tap into an existing routine. From brushing our pearly-whites, to swallowing vitamins, to "lather, rinse, repeat," daily habits have been encouraged through the endorsement of health officials and marketing promotions of consumer products giants such as Procter & Gamble (P&G).

Consider that just a few years ago, the concept of regularly using hand sanitizers was largely unheard of and raised questions about a facility's cleanliness. Yet walk into many gyms, offices, banks, and even drive-thrus, and clear squirt bottles are readily available for public use. Many people can't walk by a dispenser these days without the urge to take a squirt. The site of the dispenser creates a strong cue, the number of opportunities to use it creates high frequency, and the feeling of the sanitizer on the hands provides fast feedback. Combined with the fact that no one wants downtime resulting from illness, this encompasses all the ingredients for a perfect habit. More than $70 million of hand sanitizers are sold through U.S. retail outlets per year.[26] This little product has inserted itself into our everyday routines.

By tying products into regular cues and routines, many companies have enabled consumers to adopt and regularly use new products. "When a product truly helps to solve a problem, then helping consumers to figure out how it fits into their lives improves their life," says Carol Berning, a retired consumer psychologist from Procter & Gamble. Carol helped P&G to establish a market position for products such as Swiffer, Dryel, and Febreze by determining how to insert the products into customer routines and habits.[27]

Consider the introduction of Febreze, a deodorizing spray for refreshing upholstery and clothes. According to Carol, when Febreze was initially introduced in 1998 it was a market failure. Even though buyers thought it was useful, they simply forgot to use it. The product wasn't tied to an established occasion or routine as a reminder. To counter this, P&G studied consumer behavior and found that Febreze could be tied to the daily task of tidying up a room as a cue. It could be inserted at the end of the chore as a pleasant finale to a mundane task. P&G developed a campaign that portrayed homemakers using Febreze as part of their daily cleaning ritual, such as spritzing a freshly made bed.[28] "Our goal was to help consumers visualize how they would work with the product and how it made their life better," states Carol. Ultimately, the pleasant smell of the product was associated with an olfactory image of a clean room—further reinforcing the habit. According to a P&G press release in 2008, Febreze continues to be one of the fastest-growing brands in P&G's portfolio of household brands.[29]

Lower the Barriers to Habit or Process Adoption

Once you've done the planning to make sure that there is a window where the routine can be adopted, you can turn to ensuring that the customer uses your product the first time and frequently thereafter. There are several ways to raise the likelihood of first and repeat usage.

- **Use bite-sized time:** An executive once said to me, "If I can't get value from a product in twenty seconds or less, it is very hard for me to use it regularly." Now this person is probably an extreme, but he is becoming less and less so. With less attention to go around, it pays to get customers started on a habit by using bite-sized chunks of time and attention. Twitter is a great example of a bite-sized product that became a habit for many people because it required less time and attention than writing a blog—which countless millions have started and abandoned because they don't have time. In contrast, the commitment required to type 140 characters seems pretty low. Keep in mind, though, that you have to provide positive feedback within that bite-sized time chunk as well. Twitter does this both via the thrill of seeing new Tweets from the people you follow every time you log in and via the ego-boosting news of new followers and lists (ever wonder why Twitter goes to so much trouble to help new users add lots and lots of people to follow)?

- **No or negative cost to start:** It seems hard to remember the last time I came across a consumer Internet service offering that required payment right from the get-go. What is now known as the "Free" business model is particularly well-suited to habit offerings: the service is free until you become thoroughly hooked and willing to pay for more features.

  Even the free model is being eclipsed today, though. The abundance of too many products vying for too little time has resulted in so many products offered for "free" that it's not enough in many cases. This is why some banks and credit card companies pay new customers to use their products. For instance, banks now offer a promotion to customers that pays them a bonus for using their check cards a certain number of times in a month. Perhaps the best example of this is Bank of America's Keep the Change promotion. Under this promotion, Bank of America rounded up check card purchases and automatically deposited the additional few cents into the customers' savings account—and Bank of America matched these automated savings for the first three months. This gave customers lots of incentive to use the check card frequently and gave instant positive feedback. Clearly these banks are trying to establish a habit.

- **Automatic renewal:** Once customers pay for your product, it is a good practice to ask to keep their credit card or payment information on file to automatically renew. If possible, provide incentives to sign up for an annual plan instead of a monthly plan so you don't wake the customers up every month with a bill reminding them how much they are spending. Many Internet services offer discounts with two-year or longer subscriptions. This will reduce your cost of monthly billing administration and ensure that customers stick around. Customers will be less likely to defect if they know that they have time remaining on their subscription. If they entertain alternatives while the subscription is still valid, such options may be forgotten or priorities may shift by the time the renewal date arrives.

A *caveat*: If your product is free, be careful about collecting credit card payment information up front. This could significantly reduce your funnel and conversion rate because your customers don't trust you yet. The goal of a free offering is to gain as many trials as possible so customers can get to know you in order to increase the odds of conversion to sales, to cross-sell, or to advertise to a large community. Free on the Internet is a numbers game; volume is essential. As a rule of thumb, consumer trial-to-conversion rates for free Internet services run about 1 percent; therefore the more trials that are initiated, the greater opportunity to convert to paying customers.

- **Target the senses:** The five senses can both provide positive feedback and become a cue that invokes an already established behavior pattern. While obviously this won't work for every product, it is important to consider the role that touch, sight, sound, smell, and taste might play in helping a customer try a product and then repeatedly use it. Consider the unique musical sound you hear when Microsoft Windows is booting up on your PC, or the new sound associated with Microsoft Bing. Can you recall these signature sounds?

A number of these elements can be combined. Table 4–1 demonstrates a few key examples.

Habit Quadrant Product Adoption Examples

Time-Value Elements / Options	TIME-OGRAPHICS CONTEXT	TIME BOUNDARY STRATEGIES	TECHNOLOGY ENABLERS	MARKET TRACTION
Use Bite-sized Time e.g., Google Search	• Free • Simple to use • Repeated	• Time Slicing: Reduce time commitment • Low Time-Value threshold	• "Reward" with search results, links • Internet/mobile access • Toolbar access	• Inertia: Brain habit • Seeking
Link to a Routine e.g., Febreze	Trigger: • Cleaning routine • Olfactory cue	• Easy to add at end of daily cleaning routine	• Low tech • Formulation of product, scent	• Inertia: Brain habit • Positive reward of scent
Make It Automatic e.g., subscription renewal	• Reduces need for attention • Discount for annual subscription	• Link to future time window	• Subscription renewal software • Storage of credit card information	• Inertia: Background process-automatic

Table 4–1: Developing consumer habits: A few examples.

Develop a Frictionless Habit Path

No matter whether you have a brain or background process, your company processes need to avoid disrupting customers when they are in the middle of adopting your product. This process is similar to new-hire training, but for your customer. What are the steps to bring the customers smoothly on board and ensure they have the access to resources that can get them quickly up to speed? Unlike the sales process, a habit path process does not stop the day the customer places the order; it continues until the customer is fully functional and has adopted your product. If you end the process prematurely, customers may find the product too cumbersome and may get distracted and abandon your product altogether.

Recall the MP3 player from the introduction that I never used. By most financial measures the manufacturer made the sale (and claimed victory); however, it lost the war on two strategic fronts: 1) an ongoing revenue stream from music downloads; and 2) competitive advantage by owning the customer time and attention through the ecosystem, enabling new revenue opportunities. Where are the MP3 companies today? Either they are fighting for share in a difficult commodity pricing game, trying to play catch-up, or they have exited the market.

Walking through the entire customer experience from the perspective of attention will help identify roadblocks to habit formation—any steps where the customer has to pay attention again. This involves behavioral monitoring of activity (or inactivity) to ensure the customers have what they need. All too frequently, firms design clever and appealing new offerings that have potential to become habits, but they interrupt the habit path by introducing jarring experiences from different functional silos such as finance and service that send conflicting signals requiring the customer to begin paying attention again, with a risk of abandoning the process "because it is a hassle."

What are examples of these jarring experiences? Complicated setup or product interfaces, product availability issues, poorly designed checkout procedures, and nonresponsive or ill-trained customer service top the list. Reviewing cross-silo handoffs usually yields the areas requiring the most improvement. This is where measures and rewards typically have gaps, and business unit executives pay less attention to them because they fall outside of a group's formal responsibility.

In addition to a holistic view of your customer experience, consider your critical transaction points where time really matters. Product planner (www.productplanner.com) is a helpful crowd-sourcing service that shares best practices for efficient and effective website task flows, such as "How does Facebook sign up users?" or "How many steps does it take to embed YouTube into a site?" or "What are the best practices for Software as a Service (SaaS) click flows?"

Displacing a Competitor's Habit— How to Catch a Prairie Dog

What if you have a competitor that has customers with deeply ingrained habits or processes? To continue the Prairie Dog metaphor, you can catch them:

1. *By smoking them out.* Seek disruption of behaviors through exponential value.
2. *When they pop up out of their "burrow" to look around.* Identify trigger events and provide compelling alternatives that cross the Time-Value threshold.

Before you begin, you should note whether the customer's relationship to your competitor is a brain habit or background process. With a brain habit, switching will be much more difficult, as the desire to transition may exist but the customer simply can't change without a large trigger. Although the benefits are rational (for example, the user knows that excess weight is bad for health), the perseverance and discipline required to achieve the goal (losing weight) is very difficult. Beyond a trigger to spur the user into action, the value and rewards that accrue to the user need to extend far higher and more consistently than what is traditionally needed to exceed the Time-Value threshold to change with a background process. Let's explore these customer-acquisition approaches in detail:

Smoke Them Out: Displace through Unprecedented Value

As we've seen in the technology industry, many innovations are so compelling that users are willing to change their behavior to try them. Reasons range from significant time savings to improving the quality of life.

With the introduction of the PC, some users were early adopters and others were technophobic. However, despite the hassles and initial inconvenience, early users were willing to suffer through the time wasters of software bugs, incompatibilities, and hardware failures because of the enormous potential benefits. Early adopters respond to such triggers more easily, and their Time-Value threshold is easier to reach because they are more receptive to such changes.

Cell phones are another example of an offering that provided unprecedented value. Easy to use and set up, cell phones have been widely adopted by almost 50 percent of the population worldwide, with a much higher adoption rate in industrialized nations.[30] From cowboys on horseback and hikers on mountaintops to inhabitants of remote villages, people have willingly altered their behavior to utilize this technology.

When innovation provides immediate and visible value, customers wake up to new methods and ways of performing tasks. The key here is to identify truly disruptive value. Just because your engineers think the product is the best thing since Grace Hopper invented COBOL doesn't mean the customers will understand the immediate benefit of changing their ingrained behavior. Products and technologies change quickly; human nature does not.

Be There When They Look Around: Identify Trigger Events

For most of us, even in technology markets, game-changing innovation doesn't happen very often. So we need to explore other means to acquire customers in order to grow our business. Assuming we have determined that we want to acquire new customers residing in the habit quadrant rather than customers in the other quadrants, this involves two key steps: 1) identifying trigger events, and 2) improving the Time-Value benefit.

Trigger events can range from poor customer service at your competitor to customer events such as subscription or contract renewal, life-stage changes, and the end of a fiscal year. At these points, customers might seek alternatives, and the Time-Value threshold will be evaluated. Depending on the strength of the trigger, customer thresholds will vary.

Once key trigger events have been identified, analyze the Time-Value threshold. Determine how much time the customer expects to spend evaluating new solutions, disabling or removing the old solutions, installing your offering (including taking time off from work or other tasks), learning your product, anticipating whether your product will work (status quo bias), and weighing the economic switching costs (such as contract cancellation fees). The value of your product should exceed the price plus these time elements plus other cost factors in the Time-Value Tradeoff (Value > Price + Time Investment + other costs).

Improve the Time-Value Benefit: Reduce the Effort to Switch

If the existing Time-Value isn't a sufficient incentive for the customer to transition, the next step is to find ways to make the Time-Value more favorable. Deep discounting prompts the customer, but it can also be a dangerous game that could impact long-term profitability.

Reducing the effort and time to transition is another way to improve the Time-Value in your favor. As we described briefly in chapter 2, rather than offering toasters, many U.S. banks have developed switch kits that reduce the amount of time and effort for customers to transition to a new bank. Replacing a long, tedious process with many forms reflecting the complexity of a bank's back-office operations, most banks now have streamlined forms and processes to onboard customers. Many have even placed these forms online, making a visit to a branch office unnecessary.

Some banks such as MidSouth Bank in Murfreesboro, Tennessee, went a step further to make the Time-Value more favorable. When it opened its doors, MidSouth wanted to attract stable, high-value customers from the 12 existing banks in the area. The challenge was that these customers tended to have many automatic deposits and debits from their checking accounts, and thus the Time-Value threshold to change was significant. MidSouth not only provided streamlined forms but provided a personal coordinator as part of their "EasyMove" program. The coordinator handled all the paperwork and helped to notify and proactively oversee the transition with third parties, such as automatic phone and insurance payments. After about 17 months, the program acquired 189 new customers representing $10 million in deposit balances (representing an average balance per depositor of $52,000). A survey of customers that participated in the EasyMove process revealed that 62 percent of the respondents either agreed or strongly agreed that the service influenced their decision to move to the bank.[31]

Sustaining a Habit Quadrant Position

As you've no doubt guessed by now, many classical advertising and PR approaches are of little use to marketers of entrenched habit quadrant products. Classical advertising and PR focuses on how to make noise and gain attention. What you need once you've established a position in the habit quadrant position is quiet marketing—a much more subtle approach.

What I've found through my research and client work is that quiet marketing involves being strategic and savvy about when and how your customers are awakened. For existing customers, you want to avoid waking them up to alternatives whenever possible. However, you also need to avoid being invisible so they don't forget about the value you are providing; this requires a careful balance. If your customer doesn't come into regular contact with your products and services, this involves maintaining presence by periodically demonstrating the value your company provides (such as reporting the number of issues you solved for the customer in the past month) in periodic screen pop-ups or quick status reports that don't cross the Time-Value threshold.

In other words, you're watching to ensure that competitors, changing market circumstances, or even your own overzealous product development and marketing promotions teams don't rudely wake up your customers. You are scanning the horizon for game-changing innovations that could disrupt routines and proactively monitoring customer behavior for symptoms of defection, while actively reinforcing customer habits. Such steps involve a keen understanding of analytics and the behind-the-scenes collection of information on customer behavior patterns. If it appears that certain customer segments are defecting, then proactive communication is required.

It also means restraint and value in ongoing customer communication instead of a traditional, high-volume "noisy" approach. In fact, too much communication annoys customers. As you will recall, most customers are deliberately reducing attention and don't want to think about your product. Communications need to consider whether there are trigger events such as an upcoming renewal date. This involves being responsive when customers want to contact you, as this is a "Don't call us, we'll call you" relationship. Such actions reduce the strength of a Prairie Dog event by providing reassurance to the customers that they have made the right decision.

Organizational Competencies

Organizations that thrive in the habit quadrant are adept at using analytics to monitor for customer behavior and pending defection and have invested in the necessary tools and skills. Innovation for this quadrant is about introducing value-added offerings that deepen customer relationships and inertia that extend the core product, rather than rapid product life cycles that maintain attention, as we would see in the motivation quadrant. In other words, it is focused on gaining adoption and extending the customer use of an existing offering rather than convincing customers to try the latest and greatest. The company is in tune with trigger events that may cause customers to Prairie Dog and takes steps to manage these events, ensuring customers' satisfaction with their decision to stay.

Marketing communications demonstrate high value and restraint ensuring the company does not become invisible, while not annoying the customer. Winners recognize that customer service is integral to retention and should be responsive and adept at allaying customer concerns. Service should be empowered with the authority to negotiate price concessions and provide options to customers to satisfy concerns and avoid defection. Some firms separate the customer retention process and organization from the acquisition process to ensure a proper focus on each area. Let's explore several ways companies can sustain a habit quadrant position in more detail.

WHEN BEHAVIOR PATTERNS ARE BROKEN: THE L.A. GROCERS' STRIKE

On October 11, 2003, the United Food and Commercial Workers' Labor Union called a strike in the Los Angeles and San Diego metropolitan areas for employees of the regions' three major supermarket chains—Albertson's, Safeway's Vons stores, and Kroger Co.'s Ralphs markets. These chains comprised 50 percent of the grocery business in Southern California.[32]

Seventy thousand unionized workers walked off the job or were locked out by the supermarkets in response to the strike.[33] Many workers formed picket lines in front of the stores. Verbal confrontations and scattered skirmishes between workers and non-union replacement workers were well publicized by the local media. Moreover, inventory delivery to the stores was snarled by Teamsters Union members who refused to cross picket lines.

To avoid this confusion and potential violence, consumers opted to shop at non-unionized stores that weren't affected by the strike, such as Costco, Whole Foods, and Trader Joe's. Four-and-a-half months later, in late February 2004, the strike ended. In the strike's wake, Safeway, Kroger, and Albertson's were estimated to have lost between $2 billion and $2.5 billion in sales to non-union chains. Stores in the strip malls anchored by affected chains felt the impact as well. One Hallmark shop in a mall containing a Vons store reported sales drops of 30 percent, while stores in malls anchored by non-union stores saw a surge in sales as consumers altered their shopping patterns.

So far, this is pretty standard stuff. No surprises here. But the rest of the story shows how dangerous it is to disrupt customer habits—and worse, to disrupt those habits long enough for new ones to form. More than three years after the strike ended, industry watchers reported that the affected stores had not regained their pre-strike market share. Although the stores have been working hard to woo customers back, progress has been slow.[34]

Manage Disruption

As the L.A. grocers' strike shows (see box), anything that disrupts customer habits can have a long-term detrimental effect. David Hirz, president of Ralphs, indicated that surveys before the strike found that customers were aware of three to four convenient shopping options. After the strike they put that number at seven or eight options, and they relied less on the traditional supermarkets for all their food needs.[35] This suggests that disruptions not only caused defections, but eroded the perceived scarcity or uniqueness of the product. When customers realize that other competitive options exist, they may shift the category to the value quadrant, where price becomes most salient.

A dangerous disruption can be as simple as a sensory change in packaging; however, this doesn't mean that you need to freeze everything and do nothing. The key is to identify what you can change and what elements cannot change. Tide detergent has changed formulations from powders to concentrated liquids, and even has changed the shape of packaging from cardboard to plastic bottles over the years, yet the familiar orange color that we see on the Tide package (and that provides a cue to habitual buyers in the aisles) remains intact. If the brand managers of Tide changed the color of the bottle to green, would you be able to find it?

Focus on Customer Service

For all of the quirks and hassles we encounter with customer service from phone companies and banks, their service is typically just good enough that we find it is not worth switching to an alternative. Yet companies in the habit quadrant whose customer service is less than adequate are playing with fire more than they may realize. Remember what often looks like conscious brand choice or brand loyalty can be unconscious habit. The customer is not making an active choice for one brand over another. If your company routinely exhibits poor customer service, you run the risk of waking up your habit-driven customers. Because these customers may not actually have brand loyalty, doing so will almost certainly result in defection. They will not be willing to give such a company the benefit of the doubt or a second chance; in fact, they're more likely to conclude that a poor customer service experience is just the latest in a series of insults that they were too busy to notice. They may even be driven to "punish" the company as they project their own guilt for unconsciously giving so much business to the offender. It often results in negative word of mouth, permanent defection, and possible legal action.

Develop Selective Value-Extensions

A more positive approach than avoiding disruptions is to deepen the relationship with customers through value. Seek ways to provide value that helps the customer to continue to reduce attention and promote inertia. Remember, the customer wants to forget about your product, so ways you can ease their burden are appreciated. An example for banks is the addition of free bill pay or automatic deposits. For Internet providers, the addition of free email boxes and digital services for smartphones not only provides new capabilities, but raises the average revenue per subscriber by $20 to $30 per month.[36] Offering free email boxes creates data inertia, because a switch not only requires one to cancel the service but the customer's entire contact list needs to be notified about a new address and the emails stored on the server need to be removed— all time-intensive tasks. Bundled products also fare well, as it can take longer to switch three products than one. Consider the emphasis on triple-play bundles we see of Internet, phone, and TV offered by many U.S. service providers. All of these raise the Time-Value bar.

Resist the Urge to Over-Innovate

Clayton Christensen's evergreen bestseller *The Innovator's Dilemma* provides insight into one of the common mistakes of companies in the habit quadrant—innovating too much. As Christensen details, many market-leading companies improve products beyond customer need. So while the company perceives that it is adding value to customers,

customers don't perceive that value. Therefore, they defect when an alternative comes along.

What does this have to do with habits? I frequently see companies that believe their customers value and appreciate innovative products when in fact the customers are sleep-shopping. Examples can be seen in the proliferation of toothpaste options for fresh breath, cavity prevention, et cetera. Another example is when an existing software package decides to reengineer the user interface. Any innovation or change to the product, be it features or packaging, runs the risk of backfiring by confusing customers and waking them up from their habits.

Coca-Cola is a great example of a company that learned the hard way about disrupting customer habits and then adapted to this learning. Any student of marketing knows the disastrous story of the "New Coke." Since abandoning that idea, Coca-Cola has done a terrific job of innovating at the margins while keeping the flagship habit products of Coca-Cola and Diet Coke at the center. Sure, there's Vanilla Coke and Cherry Coke and Coke Zero—these products come and go, and satisfy the portion of the customer base that craves something new and different. But the basic look and feel—and most prominent shelf space—is retained by the core habit products so the sleep-shoppers don't have to focus any attention as they walk down the aisle to pick them up.

Most of All, Don't Trap the Customer

My main checking account has been with the same bank since college. Since that time, my bank has quietly been adding more value-added services such as free online banking and automated deposits that continue to entrench my family's relationship with them. This increases the Time-Value threshold to switch and is a smart move on their part. So far, we don't mind this entrenchment because they provide reasonably prompt service, and local branch employees are friendly and courteous. (How much does it cost to keep employees smiling?) What I have learned through my research is that most customers are satisfied in such situations as long as they are not locked in and the company doesn't take advantage of them.

Like most customers, I am opting to use these time-saving services—the bank is not forcing me to use them. The bank has benefited from more than two decades of business and not having to spend marketing money on acquiring me as a customer. I am free to leave at any time.

Most customers are reasonable and want a fair deal. However, if a supplier significantly raises fees, provides poor customer service, attempts to impose cancellation fees, or makes it difficult for customers to leave, the Time-Value threshold will lower as a result of innate flight response kicking in. No one wants to be trapped. Although such a move might look appealing to the finance department, customers are resourceful and will find a way out. Worse yet, they will tell their friends how badly they have been treated.

The habit quadrant is an ideal position for companies that respect and appreciate customers and don't exploit their position. The best position is a place of mutual trust and appropriate value-add. Carrots, not sticks (lock-in), are a critical element to winning in this quadrant.

In the next chapter we will explore the convenience quadrant, where time saving is most important to the customer. This is where time is minimized, but attention is focused only long enough to support the saving of time.

CHAPTER 4: TWO-MINUTE TAKEAWAYS

Behaviors that require little attention but significant time reside in the habit quadrant. Habits take two forms: behaviors that we follow in a routine way, such as the route we drive to work; or "processes" that we set up to work in the background, such as automatic mortgage payments. The primary goal for habit-based products is to keep things running smoothly and to strategically communicate the value you provide without upsetting the Time-Value equation—you don't want your customer to "wake up" and start paying attention to alternatives. Applying the new rules to the habit quadrant:

- *Rule:* Capture opportunities that emerge from multitasking and distraction.
- *Tool:* Create or reinforce habits through easy adoption, cues, and fast feedback.
- *Rule:* Differentiate on customer time priorities.
- *Tool:* Identify customer behaviors and routines that can become habits.
- *Rule:* View customers as situational.
- *Tool:* Reframe products to renew or run automatically, so customers can "set it and forget it."
- *Rule:* Grow by shifting time boundaries.
- *Tool:* Implement selective value extensions to deepen relationship and customer inertia in your favor.
- *Rule:* Focus on customer time to evaluate, set up, and consume.
- *Tool:* Assess the time and effort for customers to switch to and from your products as a competitive measure.
- *Rule:* Create advantage through customer inertia and time-relevant value.
- *Tool:* Smooth business processes to keep customers in the habit of buying.

5

TIME SAVERS: CONVENIENCE QUADRANT PRODUCTS

∎

"If it weren't for the last minute, I wouldn't get anything done."
AUTHOR UNKNOWN

In the past few years, U.S. airport terminals, shopping malls, and Macy's department stores have embraced a new addition: automated kiosks that sell branded products, such as Rosetta Stone Language Learning Software, Proactiv Solution acne treatment, and Sony electronics. ZoomSystems, the manufacturer that makes the kiosks, works with brand-name consumer goods producers to distribute their products to 920 ZoomShops throughout the United States and Japan. According to Gower Smith, CEO of ZoomSystems, the machines selling on-the-spot branded luxury goods are quite lucrative, generating from $4,000 to $40,000 in kiosk revenue per square foot per year in airports and $3,000 to $10,000 in malls.[1] "This is a quantum difference compared with the $1,000 per square foot per annum in traditional airport retail stores and $330 per square foot realized in mall stores," adds Gower.

Self-serve machines, of course, are not new; vending machines have been a staple in the office break room for years. What has changed is that more consumers are comfortable buying expensive, luxury merchandise with credit cards from such machines. According to Gower, the branded merchandise contained in the ZoomSystem machines often range between $300 and $500 in value. Customers are willing to buy these big-ticket items because they know exactly what they want and the information is easily accessible. Unlike a typical vending machine, the high-tech shops use custom computer programs, a robotic arm, and videos to assist customers as they select the appropriate makeup or digital accessory. One ZoomSystems machine allows customers to sample fragrances using custom-built atomizers that release scents into the air, leaving no liquid residue on the buyer. Another machine designed for cosmetics uses a touchscreen that acts as a "virtual beauty consultant," suggesting the best product for a given skin type.

The automated self-service shops are an example of a convenience offering. Convenience offerings are time-saving solutions that require some attention from the customer, but very little time. Often what the customer is paying attention to is time—in the form of time savings—rather than the product itself. ZoomSystems' airport machines capitalize on the traveler's dual problem of time limitation and space captivity: the customer may have just a few minutes to kill before boarding, and can't go anywhere. Whether the traveler has to buy a gift for a loved one or is simply feeling bored and antsy pacing the terminal, this convenience-driven solution triggers the customer's memory and saves the day.

Although the beauty and entertainment merchandise typically sold in these machines are motivation-driven offerings, the kiosk itself is a convenience-driven offering. Buying products from a kiosk is similar to buying electronics at Walmart. We judge products such as the electronics that we buy inside the store differently than the retail store itself. Understanding your position in the value chain in the market helps to determine your customers' perception of your offering.[2]

Would You Like That to Go? Drivers of Convenience

The ultimate goal of convenience-driven offerings is to help customers save time. The desire to save time can be triggered by a need for productivity or by procrastination until the last minute. A good litmus test for a product in this space is the following question: "If this product helped me do my activity faster and easier, would that hold a superior position for me or my business?"

While motivational offerings target the heart and mind, the lower-level necessities of shelter, food, water, and sleep are prime candidates for convenience offerings. This is one reason fast-food restaurants and convenience stores—especially those located in high-traffic areas—are so successful.

In the online world, a way convenience is expressed is through sites that save a trip to the local store, such as Netflix and Amazon. There are also myriad smartphone applications that tap into the desire for convenience, including those that allow a user to see what movies are playing nearby and immediately buy a ticket.

All of these approaches tap into a customer's desire to get things done quickly. But what about the times when a customer needs to get something done fast because slow does not seem to be an option? This second dynamic arises frequently when, in our time-pressed lives, we overbook ourselves, forget things, and leave the barest of gaps between commitments. When we are later reminded of a task we forgot about, we have to take the first option that presents itself to accomplish it. In these contexts, convenience offerings can shift from fulfilling the basics to fulfilling higher-order needs.

A classic example of convenience as a necessity is FedEx, a company that built its entire business model to guarantee quick and reliable delivery of documents. FedEx tapped into the overscheduled and overworked tendencies of business executives. Do you remember the slogan "When it absolutely, positively has to be there overnight"? Executives needed faster delivery in order to avoid losing their jobs.

The ZoomSystems vending kiosk is a more contemporary offering for the harried traveler who is either going to buy his daughter a birthday gift through the kiosk, or show up at home empty-handed. The odd collection of items often seen on the shelves of hotel shops—international plug converters, computer cables, toothbrushes, heartburn medication, disposable cameras, and local tchotchkes packaged as gift items—are also geared toward forgetful travelers. For that variety of shopper, convenience products are not perceived as time-savers; they are perceived as the only option, and valued (or hated, depending on how exploited the customer is made to feel) even more because of it.

Whether driven by the desire for productivity or procrastination, convenience-driven offerings are largely about speed, and as a consequence of the need for speed, they can depend largely on location.

Avoiding a wait or expediting a process has traditionally required a premium. Sports marketers have known for years that parking closer to a stadium can be sold at a higher price than parking several blocks away. Airport and convenience stores are not reputed for discount prices, especially when you need that emergency aspirin for your migraine. Price is one attribute that can identify whether a product is a convenience-driven offering instead of a value-driven offering. A commodity-driven offering will almost never win with a higher price against a competitor with equivalent features, yet a convenience-driven offering will win if it saves time or resides in a superior location.

According to a study conducted by the Computer Literacy Forum (CLC), consumers need a price savings in the range of 10 to 25 percent to persuade them to spend time comparing prices among at least three offerings.[3] What this suggests for convenience offerings is that sellers can charge as much as a 25 percent premium for speed and location.

In the convenience quadrant, the customer is often making a conscious decision that the time savings of a purchase more than compensates up for the potential downsides, such as higher price or duplication (for example, buying a cell phone charger you already own but don't have with you at the moment).

Conveniences Are Not Habits, Though Habits Are Convenient

As companies consider where their products fall within the Timeographics Framework, some may get confused between convenience-driven offerings and habit-driven offerings. Indeed, conveniences and habits are near-neighbor concepts, because habits often form because they are convenient.

However, there are several distinguishing features between convenience and habit, including frequency and predictability of purchases. The habit quadrant tends to be populated with products that are used or purchased more frequently than products in the convenience quadrant. More importantly, many habits are renewed or engaged with on a frequent, often fixed cycle (such as a subscription), whereas most convenience-driven offerings are purchased less frequently and on a random cycle. If the customer could ever say something involving your product like "Every (morning/week/year) I get myself a (doughnut/haircut/policy renewal/bank withdrawal)," then you are probably dealing with a habit.

Convenience and Brand

Time-relevant value and location are perhaps the most important characteristics of convenience-driven offerings. Brand also plays a role in this context, but the consumer's relationship to the brand is best associated with expectations of quality and utility. Buyers will perceive the brand relative to their confidence that the product will accomplish the desired results in the expected timeframe. Consider how the business buyer often rejects the U.S. Postal Service in favor of FedEx or UPS for overnight package delivery.

Brand familiarity also helps in contexts where the customer cannot see or touch the product, as with Internet or kiosk purchases. Top-of-mind concerns in such environments are the quality of the product and the ability to easily make returns.[4] Would you be willing to plunk $100 into an automated kiosk or on a TV shopping channel if you were offered an unknown, unbranded item and couldn't even pick it up?

Keep in mind that the time savings in the customer's mind includes not just the time-saving in the moment but future time-savings as well. The off-brand may be well placed and well priced and available with one click, but the customer is often considering, "What if it doesn't work? How much effort will it take to make it work? What if I must return it?"

Establishing a Convenience Position

Successful convenience-driven products are, by definition, pragmatic. The value they offer is in saving time for the customer, whether or not that time-saving resides in the function of the product itself, the purchase, or the delivery. Innovators and marketers should explore four key areas when developing new convenience-driven products: eliminate steps; reduce wasted time; structure choice to give customers control over their time; and create proximity around triggers and task flows.

Eliminate Steps: Name That Tune in Fewer Notes

The shift from analog to digital formats for products such as music and video has upended the media industry in part because purchase, delivery, and consumption are nearly simultaneous. Have you ever heard a song you enjoyed, but didn't know the name of it? If you were lucky enough to figure out the name of the song, you had to get to the store to buy it, and then back home again to play the CD and confirm that it was the right one.

Convenience-driven buyers are leading the way for faster, more accurate search in music. An innovative U.K. startup called Shazam has built a search engine to help music lovers find their favorite tune and buy it. After pressing a button to initiate the application, listeners hold a cell phone to a radio, a car speaker, or even music piped into an elevator and the Shazam system identifies the song and links the user to iTunes for purchase and download. With a library of more than 8 million songs, Shazam claims that they have served more than 50 million people worldwide with their service—an increase of 43 percent since the start of 2009.[5]

To streamline steps as Shazam does, a business should conduct a task flow analysis that considers not just the sequence of steps, but the simultaneous activities in the process. Some relevant questions to ask include: How is the customer multitasking? What time conflicts are arising at key trigger points? Can we reduce simultaneous clutter? Do they have too many windows, screens, or devices to juggle that we can consolidate into one interface or device?

Reduce Wasted Time: Help Clients Avoid Long Lines

Travelers can spend a lot of time in airport lines. Well-heeled jet-setters in particular cringe to stand around in their stocking feet while airport security ruffles through their suitcases, looking for questionable items among the expensive designer clothes and accessories. For Manhattan-based, high-end storage firm Garde Robe, this situation presented an opportunity.

In 2004, Garde Robe launched a service that manages, cleans, re-pairs, and stores a client's clothes, and then prepares and ships them when the client travels to a particular destination. Housed in a spe-cially designed, 15,000-square-foot climate-controlled facility in New York City, the clothing items include winter and summer collections, skiing gear, and expensive and museum-quality designer apparel and accessories. For clients located in New York City who encounter a fash-ion emergency, Garde Robe will deliver a garment from the customers' storage closet to their home within 90 minutes.

When customers open an account with Garde Robe, their garments are photographed and catalogued in a private online database that the client can access. The catalog not only serves as a reminder of what is in storage, it also serves as a record for insurance purposes—remember, these are often expensive designer items. Through the Internet or a cell phone, clients gain access to their wardrobe catalog and check off the items they want to be delivered to a destination.

"We take care of all the logistics of delivering the clothes to the right destination. When possible we have the items placed in their hotel room pressed and ready to wear," states Doug Greenburg, vice president of Sales & Marketing at Garde Robe. "Some of our clients, such as a lawyer that we serve in Mexico City, travel as much as 200 days a year."

For road warriors, a key benefit is convenience and time savings. As most international travelers wait in line to declare items and share the contents of their suitcases at security, Garde Robe clients breeze through customs with only a carry-on. Garde Robe serves a wide variety of clients, including supermodel Iman, Middle Eastern royalty, and Ivanka Trump, as well as stressed business executives and upper-middle-class families.

Although luxury services slowed during the 2008 downturn, Garde Robe reports that they enjoyed 100 percent year-over-year growth from 2004 to early 2008, and expanded services into Tokyo. As of this writing, they are expanding into Southern California and Las Vegas.

Structure Choice to Give Customers Control over Their Time

In chapter 2 we discussed how the customer desire for instant gratification changed the purchasing cycle to near simultaneity for many items. The implication is that executives now need to synchronize the trigger (need) with the customer information and Time-Value more carefully. I have found in my work that this synchronization becomes more critical as we move toward the left-hand side of the Time-ographics Framework (for the convenience and value quadrants), because customers want to minimize time in these quadrants.

Structuring choice is a key way to synchronize what information to offer with how to create a call to action at the right time. Ever notice how the health insurance or 401(k) benefits packages offered by your employer are designed with a limited number of options? The insurance and mutual fund providers clearly benefit more by selling a lot of one thing, but they have also learned that providing more choice does not actually make a difference to most customers. As mentioned in the earlier discussion of human behavior and status-quo bias, default options for health insurance and savings plans operate along the same logic as the default status of magazine subscriptions—we very often keep what we have. In theory, we all want choices. But when given an option to change programs, many of us feel overwhelmed. The lesson for sellers is to strike a balance. Too many options and you risk over-whelming your customers; too few and they will complain that your offer is too rigid.

There are ways to structure choice that strike a balance between giving customers control over how they engage with your firm and avoiding customers becoming overwhelmed. Letting customers decide how much time they want to spend with you not only empowers customers with control over their time and reduces frustration, but it can be profitable as well.

Safety City, Inc. is an online consumer disaster-preparedness kit provider that effectively structures customer choice. In research we conducted for them, we found that customers varied in their time preferences toward the purchase of disaster preparedness kits. Some wanted to "get in and get out"; others indicated that they didn't know what items to put in a kit but didn't want to buy a standard kit; and still others wanted to handpick and inspect every item. In this way, the buyers' different Time-ographic preferences resulted in three distinct approaches to buying disaster kits.

To accommodate these differences, a three-choice approach was devised utilizing mass-customization techniques. The site gave customers three ways to buy the preparedness kit depending on their Time-ographics profile. The first, "Go Basic" approach offers standard packages in basic, deluxe, or premium versions so the customer can "get in and get out." The second approach—"Go Recommendation"—asks customers to provide a few details about their family profile and how they will use the kit, such as at home, at work, or in the car. From those details, the website produces an automatic recommendation list with the appropriate number of items included in the kit. The third, "Custom" approach lets the buyer build a disaster-preparedness package from scratch. This allows customers to spend as much time as they want to analyze and hand-select each component.

The three-pronged approach incents more customers to buy a disaster kit because the "Go Basic" standard package provides a fast option with a minimal time commitment. It becomes highly profitable (and addictive) when customers are given the opportunity to add to their basic purchase, extending the attributes of convenience. According to CEO Phil Schwab, "We've never had a customer that bought only the standard safety kit. One customer that entered the 'Go Basic' option expecting to purchase a standard kit for $9.99 left with a $459 custom kit. Our average selling price is five times what we initially predicted because the choice menu is flexible and allows customers to easily add items to the kits."

Customers that use the recommendation list, and even the basic kit option, almost always add more items because the process triggers the buyer to think of other items to include while visiting the site (thus extending dwell time). This type of structured (but still customizable) choice provides a method that allows options based on time preference without overwhelming and pushing the buyer. In the end, customers have built customized kits that match their time preferences for this activity.

Create Proximity: Organize around Trigger Activities and Flows

Another way to establish a convenience position is by developing an activity orientation, so that purchasers buy like or related products together and further entrench themselves in your product set. This differs from offering add-on purchases such as at shoe stores, for example, that display socks by the checkout counter. Although this method generates additional sales, it doesn't encourage longer-term repeat purchases. Activity orientation creates a reason for customers to save time by going to your location. Examples include a shopping center that has a grocery store with a bank branch inside, as well as a dry cleaner, a greeting card store, and a video store, so the customer doesn't need to drive around town.

Another example is developing "I am sick" centers, where a drugstore includes an on-site medical facility, or an eyeglass store includes the optometrist who can write the prescription. The drugstore and eyeglass/optometrist examples, when combined with a convenient location, become the customer's first choice when the event is triggered, because of the greater Time-Value of visiting this center versus a competitor's.

Internet services achieve proximity in a less capital-intensive way than brick-and-mortar stores. Rather than throwing random e-stores together, a more contemporary approach is to organize along a timeline by walking the customer through the task and presenting options at the right moment in time. Consider Intuit's small-business website (www.intuit.com) that organizes products for small businesses by time triggers and flow: Set up your business (get a website, get customer business cards); get paid (send invoices, accept credit cards); manage your business (use QuickBooks, manage payroll).[6] When customers arrive at this site, chances are that one of these time triggers is driving their behavior. Presenting products in this way enables customers to find the products they need more quickly to finish their task. It also enables add-on purchases that are linked to the original task in a time-relevant way.

Sustaining a Convenience Position

Companies that successfully establish a convenience-driven product may find, over time, that such a position can be difficult to sustain without technology, legal, or real estate investments. Many convenience-driven offerings are inherently unstable because they are time-specific—you need something *right now*. As the need passes, the urgency to engage with the product erodes. In addition, superior competitors that do it better and faster may enter the market and cause the product to slip down into the value quadrant.

Despite the difficulty, there are strategies for sustaining a convenience position, and they are not dissimilar to the strategies deployed for establishing a convenience position in the first place. The ultimate goal is to be perceived as the easiest and, frankly, only option in the eyes of the customer. This can be achieved by reducing a customer's search time, reducing purchasing cycle time, or reducing the customer's consumption time. Table 5–1 highlights a few key techniques.

Convenience Products: Market Traction Examples

Time-Value Elements / Options	TIME-OGRAPHICS CONTEXT	TIME BOUNDARY STRATEGIES	TECHNOLOGY ENABLERS	MARKET TRACTION
Location Location Location *e.g.,* ZoomSystems	• Procrastination Trigger: • Gift for loved one	• Time-critical • Captive time in airports • Instant gratification	• Self-serve machines • Video • Consultative selection menu	• Location • Time-relevant value
Predictive Convenience *e.g.,* Garde Robe	• Productivity Trigger: • Travel • Avoiding airport lines • Garments at right place at right time	• Save time • Proactive service, customization to needs	• Online photo catalog to access wardrobe	• Time-relevant value • Inertia: Wardrobe in storage
Assured Time Savings *e.g.,* FedEx	• Procrastination Trigger: • Project due: Fear of losing job	• Time-critical value: Overnight delivery	• Logistics network	• Inertia: Guarantee of time-relevant value

Table 5–1: A few examples for maintaining a convenience quadrant position. (More examples at www.24HourCustomer.com)

Reduce Search Time: Reducing search time is often a simple matter of heeding the old adage about location, location, location. In short, if customers can fulfill a need right there, and the product is exactly or close to what they would have purchased elsewhere, then they are very likely to go with the easiest option. ZoomSystems is making a clear location play. For this approach to work, sellers will have to position themselves in high-traffic areas, either in the physical world or on the Internet. Such a position can be sustained with the help of long-term legal contracts, land ownership, popular domain names, or intellectual property rights to hold the coveted location.

Reduce Purchasing Time: Memorizing defaults and linking to a future event are two ways to reduce purchasing time.

Memorized defaults simplify the purchasing process so that impulse decisions are rewarded before the buyer has time to reconsider. Amazon's one-click option for fast checkout is an example of a simplified purchase process. In addition to impulse, a memorized transaction like one-click encourages repeat sales because the customers know that they can "get in and get out" quickly without a time-consuming registration process.

A second method is to link to future time windows by following up on important product events. From our market research, we learned that a big headache for disaster preparedness kit customers is keeping track of expiration dates to ensure the kits are in working order. In response, Safety City created a tool that records the date of expiration for batteries and perishable items such as dehydrated food in each customer's kit. The system notifies the customer when it is time to replenish such items, thus extending the relationship with the customer and creating opportunity for add-on purchases. With items needing replacement already identified, the auto-replenish feature makes this purchasing process easy. Who wants to spend precious weekend time scrutinizing expiration dates and hunting down replacement items?[7]

From a competitive standpoint, this mechanism adds to the customer's convenience by helping to ensure that the kits will be in working order should disaster strike. With key expiration dates on file, Safety City is in a superior competitive position to communicate to customers at the right time on this issue. Other providers would only be guessing as to the dates and annoying customers with unwelcome, untargeted advertisements.

Reduce Consumption Time: The third and final approach for sustaining a convenience position is to help the customer reduce time-consuming tasks with which they either are not proficient or that they don't enjoy.

For Garde Robe, once a wardrobe is cataloged, photographed, and placed in storage, the Time-Value for the client of moving garments to another storage option is significant, creating inertia. Further, Garde Robe extends its position by proactively enhancing convenience for its clients. It is not just a silo delivery service, storage provider, or dry cleaner; these are all operational elements (some outsourced) that support the company's mission of taking a proactive view of its customers. Garde Robe anticipates ways to save time for its clients. "We can best be thought of as a bespoke tailor or butler with a custom service properly caring for and managing our client's garments from end-to-end," states Doug Greenberg. "If our client is arriving in New York and doesn't know it is raining when she left Heathrow, we include an umbrella with her belongings, [thus eliminating the errand of buying one]. In another situation, we noticed that a long-time client's shirts looked worn. We knew that he was a busy executive with little time to shop, so we had two replacements with similar fabrics and style custom tailored and added to his collection."[8] Doug added that they even assist some clients with donating or consigning their garments when it is time to dispose of them.

The key point here is that rather than simply meeting customers' needs, Garde Robe predicts customer needs to enable time-relevant value. They utilize information that they have garnered by listening to their customers and taking note of activities to anticipate needs, thus deepening the relationship. This creates competitive advantage because this information is not available to competitors. Clients appreciate the consideration and convenience.

Organizational Competencies

Organizations that succeed in the convenience quadrant have the logistical and operational excellence to deliver consistently and on time. They understand the process flows of their customers and consistently create opportunities to eliminate steps. Like a trusted butler, the best of these firms collect proprietary customer information through analytics or through human relationships. Such information provides them with the unique competitive position to proactively understand and predict how to serve not just current needs but future needs. Consider capabilities like Amazon.com's "Other books you might like" feature as a first step for analytics in this direction.

Why Convenience Offerings Fail to Gain Traction

For a quadrant so highly dependent on delivering value to customers based on time-saving, it is a strange irony that many convenience offerings fail to gain traction because they get the timing wrong. Either the offer typically comes when the customer cannot respond to it, or the seller is not selling when the customer is ready to buy. A large part of the timing issue is related, of course, to location. A bad location cannot be made convenient no matter how useful or utilitarian the product or service may be.

Timing issues also pervade the purchasing transaction. If there are too many forms to fill out, or too many clicks needed to buy, shoppers may feel that they are spending too much time on the purchase and abandon it before it is complete. Recall that some convenience purchases are driven by impulse. If buyers have to pay too much time or attention, they will think too hard about whether they really want the product, and possibly change their mind.

Furthermore, offer overload—which occurs when businesses ask the customers too many times whether they are interested in another product—can jeopardize a convenience offering. While McDonald's has thrived by the mantra "Would you like fries with your order?" it should be noted that they only ask once. As many online providers have learned, frustrated consumers consider these unwanted mazes of add-on offers and pop-up screens to be like a rude salesman blocking their path to the door. Such tactics not only anger customers, they also take the chance that potential buyers will fall into the black hole of attentional blink or abandon their carts altogether.

More desirable approaches let the user know how much time an activity will take. Market researchers have found that they get more participation and completed responses when a status bar is included in the survey, because it lets users know exactly where they are in the process and how much longer it will take. A common theme throughout these examples is methods that give the customer control and choice over time and attention preferences have a distinct advantage in winning and sustaining business.

Transitioning from the Convenience Quadrant

The convenience quadrant can be a great place to gain a foothold in a market. However, when a customer views your product primarily as a way to save time, it might not take much for the competition to unseat you, absent some advantage gained through technology or exclusivity, such as a unique corner location, inertia, or domain name.

Some businesses may be inclined to shift to more stable territory. As we mentioned earlier in this chapter, convenience and habits are near-neighbor concepts, and for many, a move to the habit quadrant is a natural transition. Amazon's one-click shopping is one convenience-driven offering with high potential to become a habit. Once users store address and payment information, Amazon often becomes the default source for impulse book, electronics, or household purchases. Amazon clearly recognizes the possibilities, as it is extending its payment systems across the net as a service for other online merchants.

Yet some convenience products also find it possible to transition into the motivation quadrant and to expand into a two-quadrant (convenience-motivation) offering. Fresh Direct did just that.

Fresh Direct: Expanding from Convenience to Motivation

New York City has a well-earned reputation as a foodie's paradise. Great restaurants fill the city streets, and specialty wine, cheese, charcuterie, and pastry stores can be found in almost any neighborhood. From the gourmet havens helmed by celebrity chefs like Thomas Keller, Jean-Georges Vongerichten, and Mario Batali to the ethnic neighborhood kitchens that cater to the city's international communities—Indian in Jackson Heights, Chinese in Flushing, Middle Eastern in Astoria—these places are revered for their variety and quality. There is clearly no shortage of food.

Yet grocery shopping can be a huge headache for New Yorkers. At one end there are grocery store chains that offer low-quality produce and meats at surprisingly high prices; at the other end there is a plethora of expensive, high-end purveyors. For the people in the middle who just want clean, good-quality meat, fruit, vegetable, and dairy ingredients, the options have long been limited, and best accessed with a car—a major inconvenience.[9]

In 2002 a new player in the grocery market, Fresh Direct,

launched what seemed to be an appealing alternative. Fresh Direct is an Internet-based grocery shopping service available in most neighborhoods in the New York City area. Consumers shop on the well-organized site for packaged grocery items, meats, cheeses, dairy products, fish, produce, frozen items, bakery goods, and prepared foods—just about anything you could find in a typical suburban grocer and more. Once the cart is full, shoppers provide address information and a credit card to allow the company to deliver it straight to the door during a two-hour time slot.

Fresh Direct's prices are usually lower than those found in typical urban supermarkets, and users say the quality of their products is usually superior. Motivated foodies are usually going to want to squeeze their fruit before they buy them, but the consistent quality and variety of the company's products makes it a relatively easy win for most buyers. The company has not just caught on, it is a veritable phenomenon, evidenced by the ubiquity of Fresh Direct delivery trucks on New York City streets.

In its early years, Fresh Direct was a convenience-driven alternative to the city's poor grocery options. As "Sandra" says in a testimonial on the company's website, "There is nothing more valuable than time and you guys really save a lot of that for me." Instead of spending half a Saturday either driving to the city's one decent grocer or visiting three different shops to get everything they need, shoppers could instead log on to the Fresh Direct website, click once to fill their cart with items from pre-stored "shopping lists," add any extras, and then check out.

This ease is still in place, and there are many who shop with the company exactly because it still saves so much time. But Fresh Direct also offers a greater variety of products and a higher number that are superior in quality to what customers can find at the standard New York grocery stores. Cheese options range from basic Kraft American cheese slices to small-batch, handmade varieties prepared at New York State farms; produce choices range from "farm fresh" to organic and local options; and the company is large enough that it claims to buy directly from farms rather than working through middlemen—thus shortening the amount of time from farm to table. In short, it has eased into the motivation quadrant. It offers high-quality gourmet items for foodies; local, organic, and sustainable items for the environmentally conscious; and prepared foods from popular New York restaurants for people who want gourmet meals without the time needed to sit down to eat.

The company has a recipes page that offers cooking enthusiasts dinner ideas from popular magazines and cookbooks, such as Lemon-Herb Seafood Stir Fry from *Real Simple®* and Savory Pepper Steak from the *American Cancer Society's Healthy Eating Cookbook*. This comes complete with a one-click option to place the necessary ingredients directly in the customer's cart. By marrying a convenient, intuitive site with high-quality, motivational products, Fresh Direct is straddling the time-and-attention barriers of the Time-ographics Framework, and is reaping the benefits.

Complex products can span multiple quadrants of the Time-ographics Framework. In this case, Fresh Direct extended its position across the convenience and motivation quadrants rather than making a distinct shift. The positioning demonstrates that the Time-ographics Framework is not static, nor is a company or product forced to choose just one quadrant. Different customers will view the same product through different perspectives and apply different Time-Value tradeoffs based on their priorities. In this case it is difficult to separate the Fresh Direct experience by the two quadrants, because the delivery and the foodie elements are integrated.[10]

In the convenience quadrant, we have explored situations where there is a propensity to devote attention but with the desire to save time. Those who desire productivity and those who procrastinate find solutions in this quadrant. Let's now turn to the next chapter, where customers want to spend the least amount of time and attention possible—the value quadrant.

CHAPTER 5: TWO-MINUTE TAKEAWAYS

The upper left-hand quadrant of the Time-ographics Framework is reserved for convenience-driven offerings. These products require very little time but some attention. Pragmatism is the key here, since the primary element driving the customer in this quadrant is time savings—products in this quadrant appeal to those who either procrastinate or seek productivity. Applying the new rules to convenience-driven products:

- *Rule:* Capture opportunities that emerge from multitasking and distraction.
- *Tool:* Anticipate time-critical triggers and offer just-in-time convenience services.
- *Rule:* Differentiate on customer time priorities.
- *Tool:* Market around time benefits rather than other product features.
- *Rule:* View customers as situational.
- *Tool:* Focus on the right time, the right place.
- *Rule:* Grow by shifting time boundaries.
- *Tool:* Provide options to let customers decide how much time they will spend with you.
- *Rule:* Focus on customer time to evaluate, set up, and consume.
- *Tool:* Streamline processes that create time conflicts and frustration.
- *Rule:* Create advantage through customer inertia and time-relevant value.
- *Tool:* Gather customer data and preferences to offer predictive convenience; anticipate needs rather than just meet them.

6

TIME MINIMIZED: VALUE QUADRANT PRODUCTS

■

"How many things are there which I do not want."
SOCRATES

There is a locally run frozen yogurt shop close to my home in Califor-nia that my family occasionally visits. One day a friend asked me, "Why do you always go to that shop and not to one of the other yogurt shops in town?" Her question made me ponder. From a décor, cleanliness, and location perspective, the shop is on par with others in the area. If anything, it compares a bit unfavorably because there is barely enough seating when it gets busy. Additionally, the yogurt looks and tastes the same as the other stores; and all the shops offer nonfat and sugar-free options that I enjoy. We don't go there frequently enough to call it a habit, and we don't have social connections that cause us to go there.

The question from my friend made me realize that I never consid-ered the other shops to be viable competitors. Upon further reflection, I realized that we actually spend quite a bit more money at this particular

shop than we would elsewhere, and the bill can sometimes range between $5 and $8 per serving—especially for my teenage son (who never
misses a chance to eat).

So why am I gladly paying almost double the price for an undifferentiated product, with no brand, in an undifferentiated atmosphere,
with the same level of convenience? You'll have to read this chapter to
find out. (Hint: It has to do with pricing and choice architecture. How's
that for evoking your curiosity motivation?)

A Value-Driven World

Products that reside in the value quadrant either possess standard features or have differences that can be compared with little to no thought.
Customers make decisions that are almost exclusively price driven.[1]

In earlier chapters, we covered the impact of time and attention in
areas where people are willing to spend one or both. But can you use
time and attention to gain advantage in the value quadrant, where customers seek to minimize both? I believe the answer is yes—and I'll
share some time- and attention-centric methods to succeed in this
quadrant. On the other hand, you may be looking for ways to escape
from this quadrant, so I'll cover that as well.

As we saw in the habit quadrant chapter, a low propensity for attention can be lucrative and profitable. Big-box retailers such as Walmart
and Costco, as well as many high-volume manufacturers and Southwest Airlines have highly successful business models with a center of
gravity in the value quadrant.

The Commodity Trap
The value quadrant is a viable competitive position if your company
and products are designed to work here. The problem is that many
companies land here without the business model or products to win.
Without management intervention to sustain a position in the other
quadrants, many products will tend to gravitate into what I call the

commodity trap. This phenomenon reflects the natural order of things as time and attention erode or as external forces disrupt industries.

Like a rock falling to earth, one of the most precarious positions for a company is when a product that resided in the motivation, convenience, or habit quadrant falls into commodity status in the eyes of the customer. A shift can happen for many reasons, including changes in customer priorities and behavior patterns. New market entrants also create shifts. Competitors alter the perceived uniqueness or personalized value of an offering, turning something special into a target for bargain hunting.

Another reason companies fall into this trap is because a competitive tug-of-war exists between value quadrant product producers and those residing in other quadrants. At one end, companies with products that thrive in the motivation and other quadrants seek to differentiate and add value to increase margins through new offerings and value extensions. Tugging at the other end, value quadrant providers target pricey or overfeatured categories residing in the other quadrants and find ways to deliver a lower cost, simpler option.

Victims of the commodity trap often have a business model that is oriented toward higher-cost elements such as research and development and premium-quality materials. This creates problems with profitability, because these elements are no longer high priorities for a customer in this quadrant. The customer wants to focus on price; any other information is background noise. "Good enough" rules the roost.

Many firms caught in the commodity trap don't realize how little time and attention they are getting. Marketers and salespeople mistake a spark of interest for serious intent. Many offerings in this quadrant are drive-by products: the product receives a moment of acknowledgment (such as a customer asking a question), then interest wanes, other priorities take over, and, before you know it, the customer is on to the next activity.

Consider all the brands that you see in the supermarket or at the electronics store. How many of those are truly differentiated for you? How many of these products would you like to spend time with? When companies ignore or misunderstand the mindset of customers in the value quadrant, a mismatch develops between company actions and customer expectation. This is when customers get frustrated and overwhelmed by too much "in your face" advertising or other methods that worked when the product resided in another quadrant. Companies that understand these differences fare best in the eyes of the customer because they are respectful of a customer's time and attention and demand little of it. When they communicate, it is usually about bargains; something customers will pay attention to in this quadrant (albeit briefly).

A key dilemma for executives who find themselves in the commodity trap is whether to restructure the business model or the product to succeed in the value quadrant or whether they should transition to another quadrant.

Establishing a Value Quadrant Position

So how do you establish yourself in this quadrant? Innovators that work in the motivation and other quadrants are typically on the edge, hunting for the latest trend or technology. Innovators in the value quadrant tend to work with existing categories and apply tools such as the time boundary strategies from chapter 2. As I'll demonstrate in this chapter, this type of innovation often leads to opening up previously unserved market segments that couldn't use or afford the category before. Let's highlight a few case examples.

Provide a "Good Enough" Alternative to
A High-Margin Category

McDonald's provided a simpler, cheaper alternative to Starbucks with the launch of McCafé in the espresso coffee drink category.[2] This not only provided a less-expensive alternative for people tired of standing in line to pay $3 to $5 for a latte at Starbucks, it also offers these drinks through the company's ubiquitous drive-thru windows for rush-hour commuters (adding convenience to value). Although coffee drinkers don't get the cool experience of a Starbucks store, and they don't have options to customize a double-shot, sugar-free, cinnamon dolce latte, or a fat-free, extra-froth, hold-the-caramel cappuccino, McDonald's makes it "good enough" at a more affordable price.

The introduction of McCafé opened up the espresso category to a new segment of blue-collar, family-oriented McDonald's customers who may not be inclined to enter a Starbucks. According to a study by BIGResearch of more than 8,000 American consumers in May 2009, McDonald's has stolen share from Starbucks, but more interestingly it dislodged Dunkin' Donuts from its second-place spot as the place most preferred by coffee drinkers.[3]

Break Apart the Product and Reconfigure It

Another way to create opportunities in a value-driven market is to simplify a product by breaking the business apart and configuring it in new ways. Zipcar is an example of a company that time sliced the car category. Zipcar members choose between an hourly or prepaid driving plan and have access to a pool of cars to rent by the hour. Targeted to urban drivers who don't always need a car to get around, this is the perfect solution to reduce the expense and hassle of maintaining and parking a car in the city or at a university. While auto sales plummeted during the 2008 recession, Zipcar thrived. The company reported a 70 percent increase in membership to almost 300,000 drivers in 2009.[4]

The Zipcar service is designed to minimize the time and attention needed to schedule the car—in line with customer expectations in the value quadrant. Drivers use a wireless key that can be accessed within minutes on their smartphone to unlock a car in Zipcar locations around the world. This is accomplished without the hassles of traveling to a rental service desk, filling out forms, or speaking to a service representative.[5]

Zipcar didn't design a new automobile and they don't offer a differentiated customer experience of using the car—the car is the same as any other. What Zipcar did was to reconfigure the way a car is owned and consumed, removing the hassles and costs of car ownership for urban dwellers who periodically need a vehicle to get from here to there.

It also expanded the market by bringing an automobile within reach of an underserved segment that doesn't have the financial means to own and maintain a car. This service delivers time-relevant value to customers.

McDonald's and Zipcar provide just two examples of value quadrant providers attacking categories that reside in other quadrants. By applying the time boundary tools I described in chapter 2, such as time slicing, you can brainstorm other ways to reconfigure products in the value quadrants.

Sustaining a Value Quadrant Position

In addition to continuously seeking ways to reduce cost and streamline operations, there are ways to maximize profit in the value quadrant and achieve market traction. These include: expand category variety, synchronize with the buying trigger, and deploy agile promotions and offers.

Expand Category Variety: Caskets and Toasters

We all want low prices. Who doesn't want to save money? Yet we often have neither the time nor the inclination to drive to the latest door-buster deal. Although a segment of motivated shoppers will happily drive across town to save a few dollars and clip coupons till they develop carpal tunnel syndrome, most people take a more pragmatic view.

Shoppers know they may save a few dollars buying only the loss leaders from each store, but this is very time-consuming. Some academic studies indicate that shoppers do not always check prices because they believe "that the limited total savings from checking the prices is not worth the time or effort."[6]

Ultimately, the promise of "everyday low prices" and a one-stop shop across many items factors into the Time-Value Tradeoff for many buyers and lures them into big-box stores. Electronic storefronts have also followed suit and are enabling a broader set of categories. Without the need to carry physical inventory, Web-based retailers are less capital intensive than those in the physical world. As a result, these companies can carry a wider range of products. For the thrifty, Walmart.com offers funeral caskets for $999 in several sizes and colors.[7] Now, caskets aren't exactly an item most people wheel out of the store and hoist into the back of the family Suburban, but this option is helpful nonetheless for the bereaved on a tight budget. By increasing competition with funeral homes, Walmart changed the perception of caskets from a very personalized, motivational (and emotional) item that no one would imagine shopping around town for to an item that can be compared by price and purchased from the comfort of one's home.

If you find yourself competing against a value quadrant company that has a lower cost structure, you will need to compete on something other than price. To illustrate, funeral homes and casket retailers should consider options to increase the Time-Value of their convenience or motivation approaches to customers. To do so, they might make the process of buying the casket easier for the family through bundling with other services (convenience) or they might make the experience more personalized, local, and unique (motivation).

Increasing variety with more product categories (for example, toasters and sporting goods) tends to be beneficial to the Time-Value Tradeoff, and it ultimately increases dwell time. Remember the example of going to the store to buy two items and ending up with a cartful? As one overworked, self-employed mom described her Time-Value Tradeoff to me, "We go to Costco and buy what's there. My kids sometimes complain that they want other items that are available in other stores, but it's not worth the drive. I simply don't have time."

As mentioned earlier, many people are not willing to drive all over town (or to go to the hassle of registering on different websites, for that matter) to buy a loss leader. In an interesting twist to this scenario, some big-box retailers are now using loss leaders to drive customers to their online stores in the hope that the wider variety will increase e-commerce dwell time and keep shoppers coming back. Walmart's recent online price war on books was not about becoming a leader in the bookselling business. The goal was to lure more customers away from

Amazon to Walmart's online store.[8] As you may recall, most people spend a fraction of their time in online commerce, and Walmart wants to increase their share of the online world.

Similarly, in a business-to-business environment, a company may select a supplier—despite knowing that there will be price variations and that the supplier won't be able to provide the lowest price on every part—because it offers the promise that the company will end up with a lower overall net cost across the spectrum of parts. Indeed, more money could be saved through one-off negotiations with many individual suppliers, but the Time-Value Tradeoff works against it.

Although the concept of strategic suppliers for manufacturing collaboration is not new, there is also a pragmatic, time-based element to this. One study by the American Productivity and Quality Center (APQC) found that the median cost of processing a purchase order across a broad set of industries is $162.09.[9] For some companies, it can be as high as $506.52 per P.O. If a company purchases thousands of parts for its manufacturing line, these costs can add up. Moreover with reductions in staffing, using an "everyday low price" vendor offering a wide variety of goods may not mean getting the absolute lowest prices but could be a highly valued survival technique for a short-staffed, overworked procurement department that wants to leave the office on Friday evening by 5:00 p.m.

Synchronize with the Buying Trigger

While increasing category variety is beneficial to Time-Value, increasing the number of items within a category is not. The Internet has dramatically ramped up the pressure on value offerings. Today the time it takes to compare prices on the Internet is minimal when compared to the previous method of driving around town. There are price comparison programs like PriceGrabber and mobile phone applications like Save Benjis and Frucall that make price comparison possible while standing in the store.

Despite the ability to shop around, Internet stores carry far more goods than a retail store, and it is not unusual to see e-tailers offering several hundred TVs or several hundred thousand pairs of shoes. The number of choices available to a customer can be staggering. As we discussed in chapter 2, the customer's desire for instant gratification is increasing the simultaneity of the purchasing steps. Combining this desire with the fact that the customer's propensity in the value quadrant is to spend minimal time and attention, we can see that there is an especially small window of time to synchronize the triggered need with the product information and Time-Value Tradeoff. This is why managing choice in this quadrant is important, as the customer will not take long to make a decision and move on.

Manage choice in a split-second world. A number of academic studies suggest that reducing the number of choices may increase sales because customers who are given too many choices give up and abandon the process altogether. Reducing the number of products within a category, either by paring down the number of choices stocked in inventory or through selective online search, is one way to avoid overwhelming customers. After all, who has the time to look at more than 10 TVs when they all seem about the same? Reviewing TVs beyond these boundaries offers diminishing returns in terms of time and value.

For online stores with many stock-keeping units (SKUs), targeted search engines that enable customers to find only brown shoes in narrow size 8 reduce the chances of a lost sale. The busy customer doesn't have the patience to look for "a needle in a haystack."

Another element of synchronizing the customer need with the information is how choices are designed. Research has found that memory recall has an effect on decision-making and the first option presented tends to be selected more often—this is called the primacy effect.[10]

An online study by Klagenfurt University in Austria tested the choices people made when purchasing tents. Despite the variety of tent characteristics, such as shape and weatherproofing, the buyers selected the first tent presented to them 2.5 times more than any other.[11] When the researchers followed up with the buyers, however, customers said they made their decision based on some feature: it had the best shape or better waterproofing, for example. Customers tended to pick the first item presented, even though they looked at other items and believed they made the best choice. Researchers believe that the primacy effect arises because the first item viewed is more effectively stored in long-term memory.[12] This suggests that the first option presented to the customer shouldn't be the lowest-cost option.

Although customers may be driven by price, many sites make the "sort by price" button something that must be found and selected as a second step to avoid the primacy effect working in favor of the lowest-price (and therefore usually lowest-margin) option. Similarly, this is often why we see subscription services setting the default to an annual subscription rather than a monthly one. Doing so forces a rushed, price-sensitive user to take an extra step to click and drop down the menu in order to take advantage of a lower price. Although the lower price is available on the menu, selecting it entails one more step, one that distracted and harried purchasers may not even notice.

Ensure product reviews and information are readily available. No one wants to waste time on a bad product. Another way to synchronize the information with the need is to ensure customer reviews and product information are readily available. Although reviews are common on sites like Amazon, only 50 percent of e-tailers in the United States actually use them, primarily because of fear that negative feedback may affect sales. Yet 80 percent of Web buyers look at reviews when shopping online, according to Forrester Research.[13]

People are attracted to companies that receive five-star reviews, which rise to the top of search lists. Despite the weaknesses of crowd-sourced reviews, a 2009 global online study by Nielsen found that 70 percent of people trust recommendations from unknown users posted online, a 9 percent increase from 2007. This was second only to recommendations from people that they know.[14]

In the near future, we can expect to see augmented reality and more location-based services on cell phones become mainstream in the purchasing process. Augmented reality supplements a physical-world environment with computer-generated imagery in a real-time setting. Consider a scenario where customers can walk down a street and bring up a complete set of information about a restaurant, including menus and user reviews, simply by pointing their smartphone's camera at the storefront. Businesses that have their information populated in these services versus those that don't will have an advantage.

Create appropriate calls to action: the Time-Value of rebates. Obviously, when price is a key factor in the decision, the management of pricing promotions becomes more critical. Triggering customers with promotions at the right sliver of time in this quadrant is crucial to not only gaining sales but to directing customer behavior to cross-selling opportunities in order to increase margin.

Rebates are a frequently used tool in the consumer electronics industry and for other high-value goods. Consumers perceive the benefit of a discount when they pay for the purchase, but they often forget to claim the rebate later. Rebates can be attractive to consumers because such programs tend to offer deeper discounts than one would expect if a discount were applied immediately across the board. Some consumers will follow through, file the claim, and reap the benefits of paying attention. Others will forget to file, ultimately to the benefit of the manufacturer. In this case, the manufacturer was able to offer the perceived benefits of the discount without the loss of profitability from the discount—all as a result of of the customers' innattentiveness and inaction.

In designing rebate programs, sponsoring manufacturers bet that the monetary value of the rebate is high enough to be perceived as a favorable discount and worth the Time-Value to file at the point of purchase. However, they cannot set the value too high because it would cross the Time-Value threshold for too many consumers. If too many customers pay attention and file claims, the cost of the program is pushed higher than an immediate across-the-board discount.

Some firms have used customers' lack of time and attention to manipulate the rebate process by including excessive steps and requirements to earn the rebate or by rejecting submissions from honest consumers for the slightest error or omission. This is not good for the industry, nor for brand reputation, and may open rebates to legislative intervention. These programs need to be reasonable and reward legitimate consumers that make the effort to file.

Some busy customers have begun to catch on to this phenomenon and will opt for a product with an immediate discount over one with a higher rebate but more time and attention required to earn it. Others value their time differently and don't mind the extra effort for the greater financial reward. From a societal perspective, rebates are a way to provide a subsidy for goods at a lower price for those with less money but more time, such as lower-income seniors and students, but ultimately charge more to those in wealthier economic classes that may not be willing to spend the time for a relatively small amount of money. Ultimately, if your products are targeted toward busy, wealthy consumers and your competitors are all offering discounts, a rebate program may not be considered attractive to that segment from a Time-Value Tradeoff perspective.

Deploy Agile Promotions and Offers

Structuring promotions and offers in an agile way is another route to drive sales and cross-selling in this quadrant. Having the right promotion at the right time is more critical when there is minimal time and attention involved. I'll list a few options here, but I will not describe them in detail because they are well known in practice.

- **Timing promotions using behavioral data:** Mobile lunch-ordering providers that serve fast-food restaurants know exactly what day of the week and time of day customers order lunch out, where they are located, what they eat, and what restaurants they like. Promotional offers can be targeted to these attributes to drive traffic and up-sell. Elements of the mix include not just timing, but also how often the promotions will be sent and how they will integrate with other product promotions targeted at the customer.
- **Social media promotions:** Although customers don't want extensive two-way conversations and won't take time to read your corporate blog, they will sign up for specials and promotions to get bargains that you offer through Facebook and

Twitter. Also consider making shopping fun and encourage traffic like Foursquare and Gowalla did by providing promotions in location-based offers. Bite-sized promotions fit with customer expectations for the quadrant and they are a good way to connect with customers, albeit briefly.

- **Extend the timeframe**: If you are a business supplier and your customer demands discounts, you could negotiate a long-term contract in exchange for lower pricing to lock in a volume purchase. Although the margins are lower, you will sleep at night knowing that you have secured future revenue streams.

Organizational Competencies

Organizations that thrive in the value quadrant are relentless cost cutters. Competition in this category is very much tied to well-timed pricing campaigns and promotions, including loss leaders. Creative pricing in the form of discounts, choice architecture, and category mix is essential to profitability. Merchandising in the form of ensuring product information, customer reviews, and inventory is critical to a world in which split-second decisions matter. The ability to identify optimal categories and increase the category mix is important to increasing cross-sell opportunities.

Another important attribute is the ability to keep the offering simple and streamlined. Although this sounds, well, ahem, simple, it requires the organizational fortitude to say "no" to feature creep. A Zen or minimalist approach to product design and delivery is optimal. As Albert Einstein once said, "Everything should be made as simple as possible, but not simpler."

Transitioning to Other Quadrants

Like a fish out of water, most companies caught in the commodity trap seek to move to other quadrants. See the "Establishing a Position" section in each of the quadrant chapters for ideas on how to transition quadrants if you're unhappily stuck in the value quadrant.

One technique for transitioning quadrants is to identify time-sensitive value (as discussed in chapter 2). This is where you seek times when the product category may be viewed as higher value than at other times and a premium could be charged or new products developed to serve this need.

Another technique is to reconfigure the product in a new way. You may be wondering at this point about the yogurt store that I mentioned at the beginning of this chapter that had no brand, no product differentiation, and a location on par with other yogurt shops in the area. Why were they competitively superior in my mind to other stores in the area? Why do people go there and happily pay more?

Here's how they merchandise and price their offerings in a way that makes them unique: The store allows customers to serve and select their own yogurt flavors and toppings, similar to a buffet. With four self-serve machines holding eight flavors, customers are free to mix a small portion of regular chocolate along with the sugar-free, fat-free lemon yogurt they've selected. In addition, the shop has a self-serve topping bar with about 30 choices, from Reese's Pieces to nuts to chilled fruit. No more having to debate whether you want to pay for one topping or two or whether you want a small, medium, or large serving of yogurt. In this store, customers build their own yogurt to their liking. The customer decides how much or how little time to devote to customizing it.

In addition to everyone's yogurt blend being unique, the pricing scheme also defies direct price comparison. Once the selection is complete, the yogurt and toppings are weighed and purchased by the pound. The actual price is not known until the end of the process, which makes comparison difficult. At the point of purchase, time and effort have been invested in building the product, and most people would not want to invest additional time (and the embarassment) to question the pricing in order to rebuild a less-expensive mix while their friends' yogurts are melting. Besides, the customer is in control of portions, and picking yogurt and toppings with family and friends is fun. Everyone ends up gladly paying more for the experience.

Frozen yogurt shops are a motivation offering at heart, because they are often visited with family and friends. In recent years, new entrants pushed them into the value quadrant by eliminating uniqueness in the minds of consumers. This shop was able to regain its position as a motivation offering based on reconfiguring the product to enable self-serve customization through choice architecture and through pricing by the pound when everyone else was pricing by the cup. The other stores in the area belong to national chains and are not able to change their operating procedures easily to this type of operating model.

Marketers and innovators often believe that creating differentiation involves expensive investments in luxury features, heavy advertising, and building big brand names. Yet this story demonstrates that even small businesses on a shoestring can differentiate themselves and increase margins by putting the customer in control of time and product selection through creative merchandising and altering the pricing formula.

As we have seen, the value quadrant has several unique challenges and opportunities. Winners in this quadrant must continually seek ways to reduce cost structure and/or simplify the product while creatively improving profitability through up-sell, category variety, pricing schemes, and timely offers. Synchronizing the trigger with the information, call-to-action, and Time-Value becomes essential. Companies that find themselves in the commodity trap, where they are competing on price but don't have the cost structure or organizational competencies to win in this segment, need to seek ways to move to another quadrant.

We've now covered all of the four quadrants of the Time-ographics Framework. In our next chapter, we'll step back and review overall steps to innovate a product using a Customer Time-Value mindset.

CHAPTER 6: TWO-MINUTE TAKEAWAYS

Products that reside in the lower-left corner of the Time-ographics Framework are value-driven—products where the customer time and attention is driven primarily by price. Plenty of simpler, low-cost products are designed to live in this price-driven world. Still other products fall into default commodity status because they were designed for other quadrants but failed to sustain their position. In those cases, the commodity trap is a no-man's land, because the company operations and culture—even the product design—are not aligned with a low-cost model. Applying the new rules might help products that have fallen into commodity positions prosper there or dig their way out.

- *Rule*: Capture opportunities that emerge from multitasking and distraction.
- *Tool*: Architect product choice and serial position to enhance profitability.
- *Rule*: Differentiate on customer time priorities.
- *Tool*: Let customers self-serve their own product bundles from commodity components to reframe perceptions of uniqueness.
- *Rule*: View customers as situational.
- *Tool*: Identify opportunities to attack competitors' convenience and motivation position through price or simplicity.
- *Rule*: Grow by shifting time boundaries.
- *Tool*: Reconfigure products by redefining time-use for the category (e.g., dwell time, time slice, time shift) to serve new segments of customers that don't use the category today.
- *Rule*: Focus on customer time to evaluate, set up, and consume.
- *Tool*: Synchronize the buying trigger with the product information and Time-Value Tradeoff.
- *Rule*: Create advantage through customer inertia and time-relevant value.
- *Tool*: Apply time-sensitive value as a path out of the value quadrant to alter the customer value equation.

7

INNOVATING CUSTOMER TIME-VALUE INTO MARKET TRACTION

Carpe Diem (Latin): Seize the Day

In the past 20 years, diabetes has evolved from a lesser-known illness into an outright epidemic. At least 171 million people worldwide have diabetes today, including 26 million in the United States alone (about 8 percent of the U.S. population).[1] Defined by an inability to regulate glucose (sugar) in the blood, the most common form of the disease is associated with obesity, lack of exercise, and poor eating habits. Roughly 95 percent of diabetics have this "Type 2" form of the disease, which can be controlled through a combination of diet, exercise, and medication.

The consequences of such a high disease burden can be felt on both the individual and societal level: according to the World Health Organization, the cost of diabetes ranges from 2.5 percent to 15 percent of direct healthcare costs worldwide.[2] At a company level, poor individual disease management has bottom-line impacts. Eric Compton, founder of SymCare Personalized Health Solutions, a member of the Johnson & Johnson (J&J) family of companies, says, "Episodes of hypoglycemia [low blood sugar] can happen as often as three times a quarter per patient. Industry studies show that diabetic employees' total health care costs average more than $22,000 a year."

Effective management includes periodic self-monitoring of blood-sugar levels with a glucose meter, such as the OneTouch® brand offered by J&J's LifeScan, Inc. Yet Compton observes, "When we look across a ninety-day view of diabetic patient activity fifty percent of patients are not achieving their metabolic targets—that's half the patients in the U.S. that are not in good control of their situation."[3]

The challenge for many diabetics is that while most are aware that diabetes can have dire long-term consequences (blindness, the loss of a limb, coma, or, in some cases, death[4]), daily symptoms can be subtle, not always noticeable or restrictive enough to encourage lasting lifestyle changes. The chronic nature of the illness makes it difficult for diabetic patients to get ongoing support from U.S. medical providers. Disease management is constant, and it requires lots of patient knowledge, diligence, and willpower.

The inTouch™ Diabetes Program: Designed with Patient Behavior in Mind

In this gap between patient motivation and provider support, Johnson & Johnson saw an opportunity. Compton and his team set out to discover:

- What activities or competing priorities were affecting patients' ability to stay on track.
- What was the most expedient way for patients to access customized knowledge about their situation.
- What reminders and incentives could help patients maintain a healthy regimen.

These challenges prompted SymCare to develop and launch the

inTouch diabetes program in 2009. The program is an advanced, comprehensive, and wireless diabetes management program that has been cleared by the U.S. Food and Drug Administration (FDA). It's offered through health insurance companies, disease management companies, and employers. The program uses a combination of objective biometric data, education, and a rewards program to better engage patients in effective diabetes management aimed at reducing healthcare costs.

The goal of the program is to help patients better understand their condition by identifying trends, offering personalized communications, and providing healthcare professionals (HCPs) selected personalized education materials. Patients are encouraged to invite their HCPs to participate in the program alongside them to help monitor progress, set goals, and interpret information. In addition, some patients receive one-on-one nurse coaching where they can discuss their diabetes and then follow up their discussion with their HCP. Human contact is complemented by personalized educational content from Johns Hopkins University, diet and exercise programs from eDiets, and an incentive program through Amazon.com that rewards users for meeting goals and staying on track.

By asking what reminders and incentives the company could provide in addition to glucose monitors to help diabetics stick with a healthy regimen, SymCare came up with a lifestyle solution that serves patient needs within a realistic world of low incentives, lack of consistent care resources, and conflicting time and attention priorities.

Adopting a Time-Value Mindset

As the inTouch solution and the many examples in earlier chapters demonstrate, the techniques we have discussed throughout this book can be used to assess your current situation and identify opportunities that significantly add value to customers and lead to growth. There are a number of different ways a Customer Time-Value mindset can be applied. This chapter focuses on applying Time-ographics analysis to innovate a new product opportunity.

One of the biggest opportunities of a Time-Value approach is that it provides a fresh perspective about customer behavior that will uncover opportunities that may not have surfaced with traditional techniques. This approach will also help to explain barriers to customer adoption.

It is important to assess the current situation and plot your course for your desired future state. In this chapter, I'll walk through the process for performing such an assessment of Time-ographics opportunities. I'll follow the general flow for innovating for Time-Value, namely: 1) conduct a Time-ographics analysis of the context and opportunities, 2) assess time boundary strategies and tools that can be applied, and 3) drive product adoption and market traction by applying Time-Value Tradeoffs and tools. Figure 7–1 describes this flow.

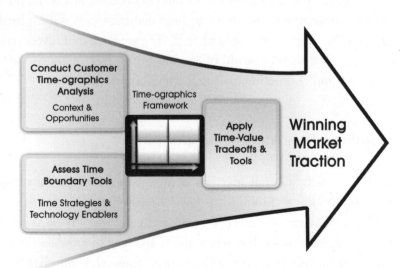

Applying the New Rules
Turning Customer Time-Value into Market Traction

Figure 7–1: Customer Time-ographics analysis and time boundary tools provide critical inputs to the Framework. Applying Time-Value Tradeoffs and tools enables market traction.

Determine Your Growth Objective

To understand your product from the perspective of customer time and attention, I'll describe a general sequence of exercises. Note that the actual sequencing and emphasis on each of these steps will vary based on your objectives. Not all steps are needed in order to derive value from this process.

For the purposes of the discussion in this chapter, we'll focus on developing a new product for an existing market by identifying whitespace opportunities between product categories. Examples for applying a Time-Value mindset to other growth objectives such as entering new markets, increasing market penetration with existing products, and identifying "blue sky" opportunities with new products and new markets can be found at www.24HourCustomer.com.

Step 1: Conduct Customer Time-ographics Analysis

The first set of exercises follow the sequence that I described in chapter 1, namely:

1. **Evaluate the context** by mapping your **products** onto the Time-ographics Framework and analyzing **customer activity** from a time-and-attention perspective.
2. **Identify opportunities** that emerge from the framework and customer activity flow.

Evaluate the Context: Map the Product

Although we are seeking to identify new products for an existing market, it is usually best to begin with a quick assessment of where customers perceive your existing product(s) in relation to time and attention priorities. Most companies have multiple product lines, so this analysis should be pursued at a logical product or service level because different product lines may reside in different quadrants. Map your relevant products that touch the target customer and note the dominant quadrant (motivation, habit, convenience, value) for each. Then, assess what quadrant position(s) you'd like to achieve in the future.

If you are seeking growth for an existing product, this analysis is more in-depth and dives deeper into the framework exercises that were described in chapter 1.

Distinguish between multi-quadrant products and shifts in quadrant positions. If your product crosses two quadrants, the next step is to distinguish whether it is an integrated offering such as Fresh Direct (motivation and convenience) or a sequenced transition of the customer from one segment to the next such as HubSpot, which starts with a motivation position (website grader diagnostic), then transitions the customer to the habit quadrant (subscription software). Does the customer perceive the offering as an integrated customer experience? Or is it a motivation selling program (such as a diagnostic) that results in a paid offering (such as software) that resides in another quadrant?

For some products this will be a straightforward exercise; for others there will be gray areas. The goal of this exercise is to look for directional information using the framework tool that helps to inform your analysis. Take note of your observations. You can always revisit this step after you have finished the rest of this process, as your answers there may provide further insights that will clarify the analysis.

Evaluate the Context: Map the Customer Activity

The second exercise is to map the customer activity that is related to your product on the Time-ographics Framework. Starting with the customer activity closest to your current product helps to focus the analysis in line with options that could be realistically pursued.[5] For example, if we are selling running shoes, we would explore the activity of runners.

To further illustrate, if we were to hypothetically apply these exercises to diabetic patient activity, it might reveal that many patients were not maintaining their regimen because of a low propensity to maintain focus on the issue. The patient most likely knows that care is important, but similar to a weight-loss diet, the propensity to devote time and attention is low because this is not a particularly enjoyable activity. The natural erosion of patient attention coupled with an inconsistent trigger of self-improvement motivation and lack of a consistent routine suggests underlying causes to the loss of attention. From the context exercises that follow, we would see that proper care is repeatable, and that the digital nature of glucose meters enables habit formation (cue, frequency, feedback) that would enable the patient to manage attention and improve care by promoting a healthy regimen.[6]

Evaluate the Context: Assess the Customer Landscape

With a good sense of how your current product and customer activity maps to the Time-ographics Framework, exploring the customer context will lead to further opportunities.

Create a context timeline. This exercise outlines the customer activity or objective from a time sequence perspective. As part of this process, identify areas where a new product could be attached to an existing routine.

It is important not only to look at what the customer is doing today but to ask creative questions about the steps the customer should be taking. This is particularly important with analyzing repetitive routines because they are remnants of past goals, and may not make sense anymore. University researchers Wendy Wood and David T. Neal found that habits typically are the residue of past goal pursuit. Once acquired, habits are performed without mediation of a goal to achieve a particular outcome.[7] In other words, the habit may have been formed in pursuit of a goal *in the past*, but the user may be repeating the behavior (or a modification of it) without a specific goal in mind.

You may wonder about the relevant timeframe for analysis. Customer time in this model can span minutes, hours, an actual day, or smaller chunks of time spread out over weeks or months. Motivation and habit offerings need to analyze the broadest context of consumption, while convenience and value offerings typically entail shorter timeframes.

The goal here is to evaluate as broad a context as possible surrounding the product use without over-analyzing. Start with big-picture questions about how your customer spends his or her time, such as "What is the day in the life of a diabetic patient? How do patients monitor and care for themselves?" You can always expand from there if it looks promising to do so.

The final element of this analysis is to evaluate competing activities. What macro-level activities are competing for the customer's time and attention during this timeframe? Are diabetic patients working on a manufacturing line or absorbed in some other activity where they are prevented from measuring or managing their blood-sugar levels?

Determine trigger events. This is one of the most crucial steps in the evaluation, because it will identify new ideas as well as pain points that will assist in the vetting of alternatives. When are customers thinking about your category? Think *big* and broadly here—don't answer "They buy financial software when they buy a PC"; ask "When do customers think (or worry) about finances?" Alternatively, rather than asking "When do businesses buy disk drives?" try "When are businesses concerned about data?"

One way to brainstorm triggers is to group them into higher-level categories. We've used categories with clients such as:

- Product purchase–related triggers
- Product usage–related triggers. For instance, can a glucose meter or smartphone be used as a cue to promote repeatable healthy behaviors?
- Event-based triggers, including routine events such as annual events or tax time, and unexpected events such as a hypoglycemic episode or a manufacturing line failure
- Life-stage triggers for consumers (such as starting a family)
- Motivation related triggers, such as:
  - Status triggers (keeping up with the Joneses)
  - Family or friend influence
  - Potential job loss
  - New management regime

- Life-cycle triggers for business buyers
- Vertical segment triggers (such as laws specific to financial services)

At this point, it is a good idea to group the triggers into three categories relative to the customers' likelihood to consider products you could potentially offer to them based on the trigger as "high action," "medium action," or "low action." How strong are the triggers?

Evaluate the sources and strength of motivation. Are there underlying motivations associated with your proposed product relating to peer (family, social camaraderie, physical attraction); power (status and greed); or personal pursuits (self-improvement, curiosity, fun, and fear). Which motivations are most salient? Which ones are strongest? Are the motivations persistent or will they erode? Is the potential product tied directly to the motivation, such as a trip to Disneyland, and fun? Or is the product indirectly linked to the motivation? A diaper is not motivational itself, but it could be tied to a motivation of good parenting. How consistently can the motivation be reinforced?

Identify Opportunities

The next set of exercises uncover white-space opportunities that emerge from the framework and customer context that we developed.

The first exercise is to look at the trigger events and context as they relate to each of the four quadrants. This is the "Jane versus Linda" exercise we discussed in chapter 1. How might we serve the Jane runner who resides in the motivation quadrant and the Linda runner in the habit quadrant differently? Do the trigger events change for them? Do opportunities in any of the quadrants look more attractive than the others? Where would we like to be positioned with our new product in the framework? Is that a realistic position to reach? How does the market size in the quadrants compare? Does the opportunity have potential to grow? Are there any options we can rule out at this point?

The second exercise is called a sequential and simultaneous analysis. For the top triggers you've identified, there are three ways to look for new white-space opportunities between categories. In general, these are the questions the SymCare team asked at the beginning of this chapter, i.e. *What activities or competing priorities are affecting patients' ability to stay on track?* Look for gaps and needs across the following:

- **Simultaneous:** Do opportunities exist when the person is multitasking? Does this create conflicts or issues? The Nike+ Apple iPod Sport Kit is a good example of satisfying simultaneous need. Other opportunities in this area include reducing the number of screens or devices in use, and linking with other brands used at the same time.

- **Identify Time Conflicts:** Are there conflicting priorities between two activities, with one occurring at a different time, resulting in poor outcomes? As you may recall from the introduction, Voice2insight addresses time conflicts for sales representatives. As Voice2insight CEO Matt Tippetts said, "With a cell phone, salespeople call information into the systems while it is still fresh in their minds. We help transform this information into CRM data updates, customer thank-you letters, and action items to push the sales process forward." (Figure 7–2 demonstrates an example of how this analysis would surface this opportunity.)

- **Sequential:** This is traditional process flow analysis. Are there gaps in a sequence of steps? This scans for opportunities by analyzing the task flow working toward an objective. Can we reduce steps to create a convenience quadrant product? Is this the correct objective or the remnant of a prior objective (via a habit)? How might the sequence change in the future with new offerings or new technology?

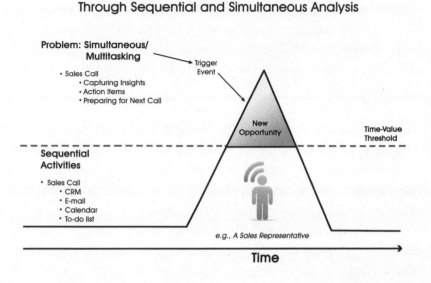

Figure 7–2: Analyzing customers from a sequential and simultaneous context perspective uncovers hidden opportunities that exist between current product categories.

Step 2: Assess Time Boundary Tools

Now that we have identified the context and opportunities based on Time-ographics analysis, can we capture any of these new opportunities by altering the boundaries of time? As you will recall from chapter 2, key strategies are:

- Redefine time use
- Shift purchasing and consumption cycles
- Increase Time-Value (or decrease time cost)

Can any of the possibilities close the gap between a good opportunity and a great one? Do any of the time boundary methods serve the customer in ways that were not possible in the past? Consider Digital Chocolate, which deployed a time-slicing strategy to open up a new segment of the gaming market. Or Zipcar's time sharing of cars. Or TiVo, when they entered the market by time shifting TV viewing. Or how Amazon integrated book purchasing into consumption, altering their relationship with customers from infrequent e-commerce transactions to a customer companion. They are all playing by the new rules.

Time Boundary Tools: Assess Technology Enablers

Although not always required, technology is an enabler in executing many of the strategies shared throughout this book. Below are some of the ways technology can be applied, many in combination with each other.

Guide customer choice. This includes the primacy effect (first on the list), recommended buys, promotional offers, and default settings. This also involves the use of technology to persuade and incent behavior.

Promote familiarity and user inertia. As we know, familiar patterns and routines help busy people to survive and accomplish more in an economy where extra time is hard to find. "Without thinking about it, you get up and get through the morning routine and get to work somehow without a lot of conscious thought—it just happens. You do it because if you had to think about every single decision and every movement that you made, you would be unable to cope with the world," states Carol Berning, a consumer psychologist.[8]

Technology creates user inertia through familiar user interfaces, stored user data, and established routines. Once the data is accumulated into a database, or the learning curve on a user interface is achieved, users accomplish their tasks more quickly and will tend to continue to use it.

Build habits and automate routines. When used ethically and for positive outcomes, cues (system bells, text messages, pop-ups) and feedback support brain habits. Routines that automate background processes help people to cope in today's stressful world so they can focus attention on what matters.

Technology can be used to automate actions and place them in the background where attention is purposefully reduced. Automatic renewals and subscriptions are a prime example. Automated bank account deposits and transfers are another. This is also evident in mobile devices that create cues and reminders for patients to take their medicine.

In order for us to change what we are already using, a product's Time-Value will have to be significantly greater. Hardware and software providers have taken advantage of this tendency for years by creating default settings that work in their favor, by cultivating habits, or because they provide convenient automatic updates that extend their relationship into new services.

Enable time preference and time-relevant value. A way to differentiate is to tailor the product to the customer to provide greater time-relevant value. This can be achieved through mass customization and personalization tools and analytics that create an offering suited to the specific individual. Consider how the HubSpot diagnostic reader is customized for the company website it is analyzing.

Another way to achieve this is through tuning product attributes to customers with different Time-ographics profiles. We saw this with the Safety City example, where they offered three choices to fit time preferences: 1) Go Basic, 2) Go Recommendation, and 3) Go Custom.

Provide a rapid innovation platform. For motivation quadrant products, keeping the time and attention of the customer is a never-ending battle and is subject to the whims of the latest fashion trends. As we saw, Digital Chocolate's technology platform enables rapid development and distribution of new products that help to manage this challenge. The partners in the ecosystem assume the risk of building what will sell, keep the platform relevant and interesting as tastes change. As a former executive of eBay said to me, "We never had to worry about whether Tickle Me Elmo would be the hit at Christmas and whether we had enough inventories on hand to meet demand. eBay provided the platform and our partners chased the trends."

Prioritize and Cull the Opportunities

If you haven't already done so, this is a good point to reduce the number of viable options into your top picks. Using top Time-ographics triggers is a good place to start. Balancing those choices against the strength of the trigger and usual market criteria such as market size and growth, fit with existing business, investment requirements, ease of adoption, and time to market will help to vet the opportunities identified.

This is also a good point in the process to vet your findings against your organizational competencies. If you are considering a convenience offering where time saving will be guaranteed to customers and your organization is not proficient with logistics, or if you want to create simple products but your engineering team doesn't have the discipline to ban the kitchen sink from the design, you might want to eliminate such options. Review the organizational competencies section of each quadrant chapter to ensure you have the right skill sets and processes in your organization.

Step 3: Apply Time-Value Tradeoffs and Tools

The final set of exercises assesses what it will take for customers to adopt the new product and for you to sustain a position with them. The Time-Value Tradeoff identifies how much time it will take a customer to switch to your new concept and the complexity of the effort involved.

This is probably one of the most overlooked elements of new product development. So often when there is the great product concept, the customer interest exists but at the end of the day, customers cannot or will not fit it into their day because the Time-Value Tradeoff is not favorable. Some element in the value chain, whether it is product design, the way it is consumed, sales process, service, or setup, does not align with customer time sensibilities and it is not adopted. Consider the challenge of serving dieters. Everyone, including the dieter, wants to succeed, but the product needs to be designed in line with the customer's time and attention allocations. Designing with a Time-Value mindset is critical.

Key questions to ask: What activities are being displaced by this product? Are these activities that the customer is willing to deprioritize? Is the customer in a habit with your competitor's product? What is the value customers see in the offering? How much time and effort will it take them to learn your product? Consider the stress level and ability of the customer to adopt your offering. Is the customer too distracted to understand your product? Can you create bite-sized adoption? What other ways can you lower the barriers to adoption? Are there switching costs in addition to time, such as contract cancellation fees? Is there significant status-quo bias? What tools can you apply to retain customers once they have switched? It is often helpful to list the time elements and the value elements separately to understand this balance.

We've discussed many of these questions in the prior quadrant chapters. Table 7–1 summarizes key activities that foster adoption and traction for each of the quadrants.

Key Actions by Time-ographics Quadrant

Activity	MOTIVATION	HABIT	CONVENIENCE	VALUE
Goal	• Capture Attention and Time • Heart and Mind Attraction	• Reduce Attention • Automate Choice in Your Favor	• Save Time • Solve Productivity or Procrastination Issues	• Reduce Cost Structure, Simplify, or Transition to other Quadrant
Customer Adoption	• Target Peers, Power & Personal Pursuit Triggers • High Value-to-Time Ratio	• Target Prairie Dog Triggers and Thresholds • Cue, Frequency, Feedback • Smooth Habit Paths	• Target Time-Critical Triggers • Solve Time Conflicts • Structure Choice by Time Preference	• Target Price Triggers • Structure Product Choice • Create Zen Products
Market Traction	• Create Reasons to Dwell or Return via Fresh Content, Custom Data, or Social Glue	• Reinforce Habits • Automate Renewals • Manage Prairie Dog Events • Use Value to Deepen Relationship	• Location • Entrench via Ease of Use, Stored Defaults • Predictive Convenience	• Always Low Price One-Stop Shop • Increase Category Variety to Increase Dwell Time • Clockwork Execution

Table 7–1: Key actions that enable product adoption and market traction vary by quadrant.

Methods for Data Collection

The Internet and mobile and remote monitoring capabilities make it possible for businesses to collect behavioral responses in a cost-effective way. Split testing of Web responses is one common example, where two different versions of a Web page can be tested to measure which one has more clicks and better response. Path testing to see how people click through a website is another helpful analytic. Eye-tracking is another mechanism to measure where the eye goes and for how long.

Wireless sensors and remote cameras in stores offer the potential to collect data cost-effectively on everything from store traffic patterns to optimal sign-up choice paths on a website. One area that holds promise is mobile tracking technologies. Companies such as comScore now collect demographic, location, and other data from mobile devices. Permission-based tracking studies using cell phones to monitor and identify location are appearing on the horizon but are not yet mainstream. Such techniques will generate a rich set of data to better understand how customers spend time and make decisions.

Behavioral techniques such as ethnographics, where a researcher observes customers at home or at work, can be helpful to understanding path flows and simultaneous activities. However, such methods are expensive to administer and beyond the budgets of most companies to get a sizeable glimpse into behavior. Moreover, they can be intrusive and potentially misleading, as the presence of a videographer may cause the consumer to act differently.

Diary-based approaches are another option, where a video camera and/or diary is sent to respondents to record activities. The camera can be effective if the respondent remembers to set it up and use it. Regular check-ins are possible over the Web or telephone, where the videos can be displayed. In certain settings these approaches can be useful, but they are very costly to administer and take a long time to research on a broad scale.

If you don't have a budget to hire a research agency, you can visit stores and public places yourself to observe customers and note their task flows. Hiring a few starving students to observe is a possibility as well. However, you need to be cognizant of loitering laws and avoid putting your employees in harm's way; some people may overreact if watched too closely.

To get a closer view, you can offer customers a gift certificate to tag along with their permission where you can videotape them for future reference. Intuit is famous for their Follow Me Home program, where their employees follow customer volunteers home and watch them use Quicken or QuickBooks. This has resulted in many new product improvement ideas such as new reports, a remodeled reports center in the software, and better linkages to investments.[9]

Avoid limiting yourself to the purchasing process. The best inspiration will arise from observing the consumption process, where whitespace opportunities between categories may appear when you see how customers are multitasking and interacting with different brands and media. Make sure you observe more than commerce activities; include noncommerce activities such as driving kids to soccer or working.

Tracking Behavior versus Asking Customers

Combining well-designed surveys and focus groups with behavioral measurement and observation provides the most accurate view of a customer's situation. There is no doubt that tracking behavior is helpful, as it will uncover what people will really do versus what they say they will do. However, we should not completely discard traditional methods of surveys and focus groups. All of these tools are helpful when combined and used appropriately; they tell a bigger story and can create the "ahas" that we cannot deduce on our own. We can observe through behavioral tracking that Helen clicked on this choice and then went to a certain webpage. What it doesn't tell us is that she had a prior bad experience with a competitor or that the competitor has terrible return policies, or the product has flaws. This is what focus groups and surveys will uncover.

Traditional research can bring out the "whys" and the background context. Discerning between hidden agendas and what customers really do becomes extremely important. This is where a creative understanding and question development are important. A good example is asking subjects, "How many hours per week do you watch TV?" Many people will lie, because they don't want to admit to how much they actually watch, or misestimate because they don't really know.

Asking better questions can elicit better responses: "Please select the TV shows that you watched during the past week from the following list (select all that apply)," for instance. Once the respondent checks off the answers, your team can determine the duration of the shows that were selected and calculate the number of hours of TV watched in the past week. Users are less embarrassed to answer, because they are unaware that the information will be used to answer the larger question of the number of hours per week spent watching TV.

Most people tend to think of focus groups as traditional conference-room meetings with one-way mirrors. While these still are needed when a product must be tasted, touched, or experienced in a group setting, new lighter-weight methods have emerged. Opinions from consumers and businesses can be garnered within a week and across broader geographies through the use of online focus groups and online surveys.

Too Much and Too Little Market Research Are Recipes for Failure

Market research will never discover everything you need to know. You need to make hypotheses, scenarios, and predictions based on your own knowledge of the market. Customers may not be able to answer questions about products that do not yet exist. How would you respond to the concept of a microwave if it hadn't been introduced to the market yet? However, we know that customers appreciate saving time, and from an adoption standpoint microwave ovens are relatively easy to use—the Time-Value of changing behavior is favorable.

Although a creative understanding is needed, I sometimes see companies use this as an excuse to separate themselves from their customers and apply their own insular views. Consequently they conduct no market research at all. Although employee and sales feedback is useful and desired, using it as the sole source of research is dangerous. Sometimes employees don't see the entire picture from where they sit in the organization, and they may also express agendas suited to their desire for more pay, expansion of their team, or a promotion that don't reflect customer reality. Although we would like to believe our sales teams understand their accounts completely, the reality is that the customers are often large, multifaceted corporations, and busy sales representatives with assigned accounts may see only a narrow, product-centric slice of the customer. The understanding of the customer is dependent upon the salesperson's ability, trusted relationship, and willingness to penetrate the customer beyond the boundaries of the next sale.

At the opposite extreme, I have spoken with companies that use market research for everything and cannot make a decision without it. Both of these examples are recipes for failure. Creating the right balance of market research and creative market understanding will result in optimal outcomes and the most creative ideas. The triggers exercise, for instance, usually can be developed with a good spreadsheet to frame the ideas and a few good minds brainstorming to conceive of the alternatives. Other areas, such as understanding customer task flows and multitasking, are often better served through behavioral observation and technology tracking.

Ethics and Privacy Are Imperative

Perhaps one of the most challenging aspects of writing this book has been the nagging issue of ethics and privacy. The techniques that I shared and companies that I showcased utilize persuasive technology and other methods to improve the customer's situation. Customers are aware and opt in to these choices because they see the benefit and trust these companies.

Customers are busy and want time-relevant value. However, the ability to offer useful services often requires gathering profiling information on what matters to them. Similarly to a doctor who can't diagnose a patient without information, businesses can't meaningfully serve busy customers without understanding what people really need. Customers appreciate time-saving methods such as preselected defaults. No one likes long registration and purchase cycles.

As wireless technology and social media become more pervasive, the amount of information about a specific customer's location, preferences, health, personal issues (such as medical monitoring), and behaviors will skyrocket. As has been demonstrated, the use of cues, choice architecture, and mobile technology can persuade and guide customers toward certain outcomes. This creates a great opportunity for marketers and product developers but also creates a tremendous responsibility to utilize and protect customer information appropriately. It also opens the door for abuse by unscrupulous providers.

One might argue that creating customer habits is bad. However, when customers are not forced, the habits are positive (such as encouraging daily toothbrushing), and if the customer can opt in, you're on safe ground. Additionally, there is a line of reasoning that doctors, the government, and public health officials should not meddle in people's business. People who hold this belief ask, "Who are they to tell people how to live?" While a small, vocal group asks these kinds of questions, the consensus in modern society is that such measures are acceptable and desirable.

I view the technologies and methods of the new rules as being similar to a hammer. One can build a house with a hammer (good), or one can hit someone with it (bad). Knowing the difference and how best to use the tool is important. In my view, incentives are great, and appropriate nudges and suggestions are fine (those are tactics that salespeople use), but pushing is not acceptable. While obvious examples such as coercion, manipulation, and taking advantage of those with an inability to understand the situation (such as children and those with mental disabilities) are clearly inappropriate, many gray areas exist. The challenge is for the industry to develop guidelines and best practices for these areas.

To tackle some of these tough issues, Stanford University has created a Center for the Ethics of Persuasive Technology. The research and practice in this area is nascent and evolving.[10] There are also a variety of practical cases of ethical and unethical uses of information in chapter 9 of B. J. Fogg's book *Persuasive Technology*.[11] For instance, the book describes a system that prompts employees to wash their hands in the restroom using cues and reminders. Although the system appears intrusive (monitoring behavior in a restroom), it is for the benefit of public health and safety that employees wash their hands (ethical). What would be unethical and intrusive is surveillance of employees in the restroom and reporting the results to the employer or using the system for coercion.

Privacy laws exist today in certain countries that protect customer information and manage email opt-in policies, but these laws don't cover everything that is emerging. It might be easier to make the blanket statement that "all customer information is private," but the situation is murkier than that because customers want the benefits that convenient services provide.

General guidelines, best practices, and values should prevail. It will ultimately rest with the business community to use this information with good judgment and appropriate controls. Perhaps the best rule of thumb to judge whether your customer policies are being handled correctly is "If you learned they were doing this to you, would you be upset?"

Businesses have incentives to maintain trust and reputation with their customers. As someone once said, "It takes 20 years to build a reputation and only five minutes to ruin it." Facebook's controversial deployment of the Beacon technology, where users were automatically enrolled (rather than being given the opportunity to opt in) to share purchasing activities with friends and advertisers, and the resulting public outcry makes it clear that such policies have a definite impact on your brand. Although Facebook appears to have recovered after dismantling Beacon, other companies may not be given a second chance.

Steps Your Company Can Take to Maintain Customer Trust

For most smaller companies the task of maintaining customer privacy is simpler because customer information and processes reside in relatively few locations. The challenge for bigger companies is that there are many customer contact points, databases, websites, and campaign management systems, and many of these practices are buried deep inside the organization. One Fortune 1000 company told me that they have more than 50 customer databases distributed across the world. If you haven't already taken steps, below are a few suggestions as to what your company might do to ensure ethical processes and to protect customer privacy:

1. **Ensure company values and guidelines apply.** Make sure they cover the use of customer monitoring, customer data, and technology that persuades behavior.

2. **Open customer communications.** Post your policy and notify customers at appropriate times.

3. **Create oversight.** Establish a person (or council) with authority to oversee and approve major changes to customer persuasion policies and the introduction of monitoring technology. But don't make this overly burdensome. Emphasize values, training, and agility—not bureaucracy and glacial approval processes.

4. **Conduct periodic evaluations of your customer facing systems and customer data controls.** Do you know what they are? How are your customers notified? Do your systems provide incentives? Nudges/suggestions? Or pushes? Do the nudges and suggestions fit with your corporate values, brand identity, and cultural norms for the country in which they are being used? If possible, hire an objective third party to evaluate.

5. **Create employee awareness.** Do employees know the laws on the use of customer information? Do they have access, training, and knowledge of guidelines for appropriate and inappropriate uses?

6. **Do your metrics and reward systems line up?** How often have we seen a major corporate program fail when a front-line employee acts differently to meet a monthly quota? Ensure everything works top to bottom.

Identifying values will be one of the most important drivers to engendering trust in your organization. A senior executive in a major Silicon

Valley firm perhaps described the role of values best: "It is impossible to predict every action that an employee could do that is wrong . . . But we can guide his or her actions through the value of 'Do the right thing.'"

This chapter explored how Time-ographics analysis generates fresh ideas for product innovation and hones the concept to gain market adoption in line with customer time and attention priorities. We also explored how Johnson & Johnson's SymCare team is diligently working on relevant and tough issues that have been historically difficult to solve because of the scarcity of customer time and attention. This type of innovative solution would not have been evident with traditional market and competitive analysis.

As we've seen throughout this book, a Customer Time-Value mindset can provide fresh opportunities. In the next and final chapter, we'll look ahead at what the future holds for the 24-Hour Customer. What will the evolving technology and marketing landscape mean for addressing customers in a time-starved world?

8

THE FUTURE OF THE 24-HOUR CUSTOMER

Tempus neminem manet (Latin): Time waits for no one

On a recent visit to Cisco, my host escorted me into a conference room where two other Cisco employees awaited us. The room had the usual accoutrements of black leather chairs, pads of paper, and a conference table, but there was something very different about this particular room. The two other people in our meeting weren't actually there. Across the table from me was a semi-oblong screen that ran the length of the room with three small cameras pointed back at me. The two other people in our meeting were sitting in similar rooms at a different location. Their images were so vivid and lifelike, it felt as if they were physically present.

While the widespread use of videoconferencing tools like the one I experienced at Cisco is a relatively new phenomenon, the concept of videoconferencing has been around for more than a century. As early as April 1891, Alexander Graham Bell recorded conceptual notes that discussed "the possibility of seeing by electricity," and an early prototype of a Picturephone was shown by AT&T at the 1964 New York World's Fair.[1] The videoconferencing facilities that existed during the 1990s were more distracting than helpful as low-bandwidth communication networks generated jerky, distorted images and delayed voice responses.[2] The Time-Value Tradeoff for most people at the time led them to ignore videoconferencing facilities. They were too cumbersome and "just not worth the trouble" to use on a regular basis.

Cisco's TelePresence and similar products from other providers are now making videoconferencing a reality as the Time-Value Tradeoff rapidly changes. One reason is that the time required for travel has increased since 2001 because of fewer flights, more delays, and the inevitable security hassles. But the value is also increasing as the quality of videoconferencing technology improves and the tools become easier to use. The combination of these two Time-Value elements with the trigger of the 2008 economic downturn, during which companies sought to reduce travel costs, resulted in the perfect trifecta—many companies began to adopt and deploy these systems.

Cisco executives believe TelePresence has a dramatic, positive impact on productivity. Rather than spending—and, arguably, wasting—time in transit, executives now have "long days" for global executive meetings. On those days, the meetings often start as early as 4:00 or 5:00 a.m. Pacific time to accommodate Europe and run as late as 9:00 to 10:00 p.m. Pacific time with Asia coming online.[3] Unlike telephone conference calls in which the audience is often multitasking with emails and other work, TelePresence fosters attention to the meeting because attendees are visible to everyone else.

TelePresence and many other technology innovations are altering customer time and attention allocations and priorities. Let's look at what lies ahead for the 24-Hour Customer and how that will affect the strategies you employ to take advantage of a Customer Time-Value mindset.

Time Zone Barriers Continue to Crumble

Technologies like Cisco TelePresence reduce barriers associated with geographic differences and affect our routines and behaviors. In the future, we can expect new technologies and methods that will continue to alter the boundaries of time. Remote services will continue to evolve and improve, from telemedicine to appliance repair. Aiding this will be not only improved telecommunications but remotely controlled robotics.

Many in the industry believe that robotics today is where the computer industry was around 1980, poised to affect our daily lives in ways we cannot yet fully imagine. Bill Gates himself describes it this way: "I can envision a future in which robotic devices will become a nearly ubiquitous part of our day-to-day lives . . . We may be on the verge of a new era when the PC will get up off the desktop and allow us to see, hear, touch and manipulate objects in places where we are not physically present."[4]

Although the use of robotics affecting daily consumer routines is nascent, perhaps the best example is the Roomba vacuums that reduce the need to devote attention to part of our cleaning routines by performing it automatically for us. In the future, as customers carve out more time and attention for the things that matter, we can expect to see more commercial robotic devices and technologies that attach to mundane daily and weekly routines. Such technologies become quiet but powerful extensions of ourselves—acting as agents of our existence.

Perhaps one of the best examples of the tremendous changes taking place in remote robotics is through the U.S. military use of remote-controlled drones in the war on terrorism. The U.S. military fields 7,000 unmanned drones in the air, such as the Predators that fire missiles into Pakistan, and roughly another 12,000 on the ground, including the Packbots that hunt for roadside bombs in Iraq.[5] From a base outside Las Vegas, Nevada, U.S. soldiers can fight practically anywhere in the world. Working the same 12-hours-per-day, seven-days-a-week shifts as soldiers in a war zone, these pilots remotely control unmanned reconnaissance and military fighting machines located in far-flung locations such as Afghanistan via video monitors.

After a hard day in online battle, these soldiers return to their homes to watch their kids' soccer games and to rest in their own beds. Yet these experiences feel as real as an in-person event. One fighter pilot, well trained to fly F–15s or A–10s, recalls that the action felt so intense that when his drone 1,000 miles away was about to crash, he instinctively reached for the ejection seat.[6] Some drone controllers also experience the same psychological effects of war, including post-traumatic stress disorder.[7]

It is not new that businesses deliver remote services via the telephone and Internet; however, the implications of remote-controlled techology will continue to alter the boundaries of time because businesses will be able to control physical activities in remote locations, not just virtual ones. In the case of the military drones, the concept of troop deployment has dramatically changed. There are similar implications for the deployment of business service teams and channels of distribution.

Technology That Manages Time and Attention Allocations Will Continue to Evolve

With the downsides of multitasking now becoming understood, electronic tools are emerging that help customers to minimize distraction and focus their time better. This will continue to alter customer time and behavior patterns. One tool that I tested in the writing of this book is RescueTime (www.rescuetime.com). This free online service automatically monitors PC usage to improve productivity without much setup time or intervention by the user. Unlike most diary systems that are cumbersome and create a Hawthorne effect, where the users act differently because they are being measured, RescueTime automatically monitors where attention is spent in active PC screen time. To make adoption simple, it comes equipped with predefined categories such as productive applications (MS Word and PowerPoint) or distracting applications (such as social networking or Web surfing). It also helps users to reduce online addictions to social networks and Internet surfing by popping up a cue dialog box when a user-defined time limit is exceeded. Users can define "focus time"; the application turns off email and other distracting communications for a specified period.

Like RescueTime, systems in the future will be more intelligent and proactive in understanding the time and attention of the user. Microsoft's research lab, for instance, has built a prototype application that analyzes a user's behavior and holds in-bound messages until it believes the user is ready to pay attention.[8] More and more applications will be able to take advantage of data stored in users' electronic calendars to determine the best time to serve up (or limit) new information.

Measuring Behavior in New Ways

No review of coming technology would be complete without discussing the ever-growing number of sensors in our environment. More and more sensors are being embedded into practically every product that uses electricity (and some that don't). These sensors allow for remote detection of any change in the environment—allowing remote health diagnostics, for instance. It's this sensor ubiquity that IBM references when it refers to a "Smart Planet." The increased presence of these sensors will improve the quality and time-relevant value of products and information available to customers.

Of course, these sensors will also enable more and more companies to gain an even better understanding of both how their products are used and of the behaviors a customer is engaged in when the product is in use—in short, Time-ographics. Such data will also revolutionize behavioral offers such as "Other buyers of this item also bought." These offers currently work better than many alternatives, but they do not do as much as they could. They capture only what the customer is looking for; they do not yet capture why the customer is looking for it, in how much of a hurry, and with how much attention.

"Yet" is the critical word in that sentence. Sensor technology can deliver incredible amounts of information. Sensors under the floor tiles in a store, for example, could detect the pathways and pace of different customers in a store. Similarly, store camera technology is progressing to capture and index customer behavior more easily and less expensively. By detecting how quickly or slowly the customers move, market researchers could gauge the customers' time pressure and merchandise items according to those needs.

Moving from brick-and-mortar stores to the Internet, the same kind of strategic developments are already in play. Web analytics that track user paths and clicks are prevalent today. Using these analytics, we can determine the amount of time a user spends per page and the path the user takes across the Web, and, in the process, create a context for what the person is doing. In the future, such technology may take into account the urgency with which users are surfing and may even be able to tell if a customer is distracted or multitasking on multiple websites or TV—something Web analytics today cannot fathom.

Further, facial recognition technology is emerging that extends beyond surveillance, and it is being used to sense emotions and happiness via the simple webcam on a PC. Unlike verbally driven focus groups today, market researchers will be able to deploy qualitative research on a broad scale that uses facial recognition algorithms to analyze behavioral reactions and emotions to online advertisements or product prototypes. Similarly, we can expect to see tools deployed on smartphones and other mobile devices that enable cost-effective behavioral capture of routines, time use, and task flows.

Trust Is Key

Technology will not be the constraining factor in collecting behavioral information. Instead, trust will determine how much these technologies will be used for innovation and marketing purposes. Abuses by the industry would lead to a public outcry and government sanctions, thus limiting benefits for everyone. Faced with businesses trying to gather data at every turn, many people will attempt to create a secured "information sanctum" around their personal data and preferences. Customers will seek to control who has access.

Despite—and, perhaps, because of—the advances described in this chapter, time and attention will continue to command a premium in the future. Customers will continue to seek time-relevant products to satisfy their needs, yet businesses will need customer information in order to tailor such solutions. Customers will ultimately decide which companies will have access to their data in order to serve them. Such decisions will be based on one of the most valuable elements in a time- and attention-starved world: trust.

Companies allowed access into the customer's information sanctum will be able to build and hold a competitively privileged position. Companies in such a position will seek to extend dwell time with time-adjacent offerings in order to grow. Apple holds such a position today with the iPhone and iTunes. While these products' platforms originated in music, they are now expanding into time-adjacent markets—such as movies—that capture a greater share of customer leisure time and block competitors. Consider the amount of behavioral information available to Apple via its various platforms. Apple has comprehensive access to customers' behavioral interests and trends that other competitors and content providers in the ecosystem do not enjoy. Apple's unique information access allows it to better focus its development and partnering efforts and then channel those efforts—for instance, as the top results in its App Store or Genius playlists. By garnering proprietary customer data to which no other vendor has access, companies can deploy predictive convenience (similar to Garde Robe in chapter 5) to serve customers better than the competition.

In the future, competitive advantage for many industries may have more to do with access to customer data that drive time-relevant, personalized products holding high Time-Value benefits than other differentiators. Companies that play by the old rules will be left standing outside the customer information sanctum, trying to penetrate but without meaningful customer information to deliver what customers really need at the time they need it. There will always be only 24 hours in the day, and customers cannot and will not meaningfully interact with every business from which they buy. Time and attention will continue to be the scarcest resource, and customers will be in more control of their priorities and information than ever.

What You Can Do to Get Started

We've explored many Customer Time-Value approaches and concepts in this book: the Time-ographics Framework and analysis (including triggers and simultaneous context), Time-Value Tradeoffs, and how strategies such as shifting time boundaries provide options for new business models and products. Many companies are already using the forces of time and attention to grow market share, penetrate new markets, and sustain momentum by synchronizing with customer time and attention constraints. You can visit my website at www.24HourCustomer. com and check out my blog for new case studies and new examples of companies that are winning the war for time and attention.

So how can *you* get started? Chapter 7 provides a playbook for applying the new rules to your products and services. You may already see some potential applications of the new rules, with the Time-ographics Framework, and other ideas you've read. While you've been reading, you've probably thought of several Time-Value Tradeoffs and how you can shift them in your favor for your company. Undoubtedly, you can take advantage of the low-hanging fruit you find.

But perhaps the most important thing you can do is take a step back and think holistically about the new rules beyond just point applications—a particular program or silo. The real win comes from applying a Customer Time-Value mindset across your entire value chain to create breakthrough opportunities. The companies that profit most from time and attention will be those that apply the new rules systematically. They will think about time and attention at every stage, from product development, to packaging and pricing, to sales, to consumption, to customer service, to end-of-life. They will apply the strategies shared in this book to innovate breakthrough offerings that encompass new business models and enter new markets.

As you have realized by now, the new rules aren't about subtle tweaks to your marketing messages, customer service, or customer experience. They are about fundamentally rethinking what matters to customers, how they perceive value, and where you fit into a world of increasingly scarce time and attention. Here are some bigger-picture exercises to get you started.

Conduct a portfolio analysis. Map your entire product portfolio on the Time-ographics Framework: Plot the products by the two most dominant quadrants. Where do they tend to reside on the Framework? Are there concentrations in certain areas suggesting that your company's products tend to fall into one quadrant over others? Is the mix optimal for you? If not, where would you like to be? Are there products in the value quadrant that you need to either cull or change? Would simplifying a category by shifting time boundaries (e.g., time slicing) present unserved customer possibilities? Are there any products that span multiple quadrants?

How do your organizational competencies align with those portfolios? How does your growth in new products (via either organic or mergers-and-acquisitions methods) align with those competencies?

Review Table 7–1. Are you pursuing the right actions for product adoption and market traction relative to the placement of your products on the framework? How does your organization approach this across the value chain?

Identify the Time-Value Tradeoffs and triggers for your top products. How easy is it for competitors to lure your customers away? Are there specific trigger points when you are vulnerable to competitive threats such as renewals? What can you do to counter this threat?

What is the Time-Value threshold and quadrant position(s) for customers you would like to acquire? Can you capitalize on trigger vulnerabilities of your competitors?

Consider customer-centric ecosystems. Companies can extend the value they bring to the customer by linking with adjacent vendors or brands to create an entire customer ecosystem. I think of this as being like a comfortable "cocoon" that is formed around the customer activity flow. It's like dwell time on steroids, as this extends beyond a traditional retail store or product and conforms to customer behaviors and process. Consider the amount of time that runners now spend on the Nike+ website in communities, races, tracking progress, and buying relative to the act of simply buying the shoe in the past. Johnson & Johnson's

SymCare extends their relationship with customers beyond the glucose meter to encompass virtually all of their daily management of their condition. We can expect the e-readers and tablets to expand capabilities beyond simply displaying information by adding interactive capabilities and multimedia support. Technology enables and enhances these connections with cross- and up-sell opportunities. In the future we can expect to see more complex, seamlessly integrated mobile, Internet, and physical offerings work together into customer-centric ecosystems.

Mobile expands these capabilities. Consider the integrated capabilities of your BlackBerry or iPhone. A downloaded Google Map linked to the device's GPS allows you to easily get to your business meeting at noon, find a local bar to meet a friend at six, play a game or listen to music for half an hour while you wait for the 8:30 a.m. commuter train, and read the daily news on your ride home. Today, all of these scenarios are possible through your own search initiative, but imagine a service that coordinated with your calendar and served your work, dining, and entertainment options proactively—a kind of life concierge. When executed well, these ecosystems can overcome the boundaries between different offerings, overcome the boundaries between a customer's work and leisure time, and expand the available selling opportunities because buying can be placed in the context of customer activity.

These ecosystems offer competitive advantages. As we saw with the Webkinz example in the introduction, dominating a window of time blocks customers from the competition. Companies that run an ecosystem will be in the best position to anticipate customer needs and receptivity to offers, and they will be the ones allowed access inside the customer information sanctum. Most importantly, though, the companies that hold the customer relationship and data will also be able to determine which companies play in their customer-centric ecosystem and what products their customers will see, and thus have leverage over pricing and margins for those who participate. Consider Apple's position today.

So ask yourself, do your customers trust you enough to share information about their behaviors? What are you doing to capture and analyze such information? Are you in a position to begin creating an ecosystem? If not, do you have strong alliances with partner firms that could?

Conduct a customer time and attention audit across your entire customer experience. Are you creating habit paths that facilitate adoption? Or are the functional silos sending disjointed and conflicting messages to your customers? How might you change this to improve coordination and improved communication?

Benchmark marketing and sales relative to customer time. Take your marketing and sales annual budgets and divide the total by the number of annual minutes customers spend researching and buying products (from Figure I–1 in the introduction). How many dollars per minute of customer time does your company spend?

Here are some other key questions to ask: For the time customers spend with you and your industry, are the marketing collateral and sales efforts that you provide the most effective? If you stack your collateral for a typical sales cycle end-to-end for a few different customer types, how long would it take the customers to read all of it? Is this significantly more than the time they realistically allocate to your company? Is there a way to make the information more focused, personal, and time relevant for the customers? Are your sales teams equipped to use the customers' time most effectively with tailored information?

Evaluate category innovation possibilities. Review the time boundary innovation strategies in chapter 2. Can any of these business models be applied to your situation? Do any generate game-changing business opportunities?

Whether you are growing an existing offering or are innovating new opportunities, I will leave you with three summary points about Customer Time-Value mindsets:

1. Customers allocate their time and attention priorities. Time-Value Tradeoffs factor into most, if not all, customer decisions today.
2. Rather than fight time and attention barriers, savvy companies harness the forces of time and attention to compete and build advantage.

3. Customer Time-Value mindsets provide a fresh perspective that can uncover opportunities for products, customer service, and competitive advantage in line with customer realities. Time and attention are scarce. Do you want to let your competitors control the land-grab for time and attention? Or do you want to proactively take control of your destiny?

Staking a claim on your customers' precious time and attention will require some focused attention of your own. So, close the book; turn off your landline phone, cell phone, fax machine, computer, iPod, Twitter stream, TV, and satellite radio; and shut the door of your office. Start thinking about all the ways that time and attention can become your advantage in the marketplace of the future.

No doubt, advancements in technology will continue to affect customer routines. It will create triggers that disrupt the status quo, and form white-space opportunities for savvy companies to apply the new rules. Yet, despite disruptive changes driven by innovations in technology and business paradigms, two eternal rules still serve as guideposts to our decision-making: human nature is unchanging, and there will always be 24 hours in a day.

IN GRATITUDE

I have to admit that writing is not easy for me. After more than 20 years as an executive in high-tech, I am accustomed to collaborating with others in a rapidly changing, fast-paced environment rather than sheltering myself from all distraction in order to record my thoughts in solitude. Despite the challenges of communicating via the written word, perhaps one of the most unexpected but pleasant surprises to come out of this marathon was the outpouring of support from people throughout this process. I owe my deepest gratitude to those who gave many hours of their precious time in support of this book. These new and old relationships made this endeavor satisfying and worthwhile.

This all would not have been possible without the assistance of my fellow consultants, colleagues, and clients. Although there are many not mentioned here that have helped along the way, I would like to specifically recognize Ping Hao, Lang Anh Pham, Elizabeth Macken, Juletta Broomfield, David Stubbs, Jim Chow, Cynthia Lucido, Louise Henriksen, Peter Van der Fluit, Kim Johnston, Ted Monk, Cassie Moren, Liz Seidner Davidoff, Dennis Wong, Laura Lilyquist, and Alan Michaels, who read all or part of my manuscript or provided feedback on my concepts as they evolved. I appreciated the candid feedback when the copy or concept either hit (or missed) the mark. It is only through such interactions that a work improves. I am also deeply appreciative of Kathryn Ullrich, author of *Getting to the Top*, who was in the process of writing her own book at the same time. It was great to share ideas and best practices with each other as we encountered new challenges as first-time authors. I also would be remiss not to mention Ana Martinez, my research assistant, who devoted many hours in support of this endeavor.

I greatly appreciate the many business executives, industry experts, and academics who gave their time for interviews and background research for the book. Although there were many contributors, a few that were especially responsive and helpful include Trip Hawkins, Digital Chocolate; Joe Skorupa, RIS News and Retail Industry; Eric B. Compton and Stephanie Wenstrup of SymCare; Roy Albiani, J&J; Clare Gillan, IDC; Dharmesh Shah, HubSpot; Phil Schwab; Brad Whitworth, Cisco Systems; Doug Greenberg of Garde Robe; Carol Berning, consumer psychologist; Gower Smith, ZoomSystems; Matt Tippetts, Voice2insight; Margarita Quihuis and Mark Nelson of the Stanford University Persuasive Technology Lab; Wendy Wood, PhD; and Jeff Housenbold, Shutterfly. I would like to especially thank Janice Chaffin for her time in developing the Foreword and for her unwavering support of this project as it evolved over the past several years. Janice has served as an inspirational leader and mentor over the past 20 years and I have learned a lot from her. I am also deeply indebted to my former colleagues from HP, where I had the opportunity to learn, be inspired, and form the foundation for many of the practices that I utilize today.

I am very fortunate and privileged to have a top-notch team of editorial support. Specifically, I would like to thank my editor, Matt Inman, and executive editor, Hollis Heimbouch, at Harper Business, who supported me all along the way. I also appreciate Tim Ogden and Laura Starita of Sona Partners, who collaborated with me by not only keeping me on schedule with gentle nudges, but also coaching me on how to structure my three-dimensional concepts on paper.

I am deeply grateful to those who aided me along this path by believing in my early book concepts. Specifically, Angie Lee and Sarah Rainone, who brought my book idea to the attention of Harper Business for publishing consideration. Many thanks to Jan King and Sam Horn for providing education on the publishing process and encouraging me to pursue a commercial publishing route with my ideas. I am indebted to C. Leslie Charles for editing my early book proposal. I am also grateful to Andrea Butter, coauthor of *Piloting Palm,* and the other authors who provided helpful advice to me.

Nothing is possible without the strong support of family and friends. I am especially thankful to my immediate family: My husband, Len, who not only provided loving, consistent support but also was a great resource for answering my toughest technical questions. My children, Kevin and Nicole, for their patience, love, and willingness to assist where necessary. I appreciate the ideas and support from the rest of my family and good friends as well. This has been a time-consuming challenge, but it is through such a process that I realize that I am fortunate to be surrounded by so many resourceful, smart, and caring people.

—Adrian C. Ott

APPENDIX:
COMPANIES FEATURED IN
THE 24-HOUR CUSTOMER

Accenture[*]
AKQA
Albertson's
Alexa
Amazon
Apple
APQC
Ask
AT&T
Avelle
Bank of America
Barnes & Noble
BIGResearch
BigStage
BlackBerry
Burst Media
Cisco
CMO Council
Coca-Cola
Comcast
Comscore
Costco

CRE
DailyLit
Deloitte
Digital Chocolate
Disney
Dunkin Donuts
EA
eBay
Ebates.com
Facebook
FDIC
FedEx
Forrester
Foursquare
Fresh Direct
Friendster
Frucall
Ganz (Webkinz)
Garde Robe
Geocache
Glassdoor.com
GM (OnStar)

---

[*] Company and product names mentioned herein are the trademarks or registered trademarks of their respective owners.

Google

Gowalla

Hershey (Reese's)

HP

HubSpot

Hulu

IBM

IDC

Intuit

J. Sainsbury

Jiffy Lube

Johnson & Johnson

Kraft

Kroger (Ralphs)

LinkedIn

Macys

Mary Kay

MasterCard

McDonald's

Microsoft

MidSouth Bank

Motorola (RAZR)

MySpace

Netflix

Nielsen

Nike

Nintendo

P&G

Panera

Path Intelligence

Pointer Media Network

PriceGrabber

PrimeSense

Proactiv

Product Planner

RescueTime

Rosetta Stone

Safety City

Safeway

Save Benjis

Shazam

Six Degrees

SocialNet

Sony

Southwest

Starbucks

Symantec

TiVo

TouTube

Trader Joe's

Twitter

Ty (Beanie Babies)

UPS

VirtualHeroes

Vive

Voice2insight

Volkswagen

Walmart

Washington Mutual

Weight Watchers

Wherigo

Whole Foods

Yahoo!

YouTube

ZillionTV

Zipcar

ZoomSystems

NOTES

Introduction

1. Based on interview with Matt Tippetts, CEO of Voice2insight, October 21, 2009, and subsequent follow-up communications.
2. John B. Horrigan, "Online Shopping," *Pew/Internet American Life Project Report*, February 13, 2008. http://www.pewinternet.org/Reports/2008/Online-Shopping.aspx.
3. "American Time Use Survey—2008," U.S. Bureau of Labor Statistics, June 24, 2009. http://www.bls.gov/tus/. These figures include both online and traditional retail shopping. They do not include travel time to and from a store. In using these figures to calculate percentage of waking time spent shopping, the author assumes eight hours average daily time spent asleep (16 waking hours).
4. Ibid. Table A–1, American Time Use Survey for 2008, includes breakdowns by activity. For 2007 from the U.S. Bureau Time Use Survey, 2007, U.S. Bureau of Labor Statistics, Weekend Leisure and Sports (calculated as follows) average hours 6.37 divided by Weekend Purchasing Goods and Services .88 = 7.24 times; Weekday Leisure and Sports average hours 4.57 divided by Weekday Purchasing Goods and Services .74 = 6.18 times; Weekend and Holiday Household hours 2.19 divided by Purchasing Goods and Services .88 = 2.49 times; Weekday Household average hours 1.69 divided by .74 = 2.28 times.
5. Exponential Edge Inc. statistical analysis of data from the following sources: "American Time Use Survey—2008" U.S. Bureau of Labor Statistics, June 24, 2009. http://www.bls.gov/tus/. The data are for Americans ages 21 to 65 years old; Multinational Time Use Study, Versions World 5.5.3, 5.80, and 6.0. Released March 26, 2009. Created by Jonathan Gershuny and Kimberly Fisher, with Evrim Altintas, Alyssa Borkosky, Anita Bortnik, Donna Dosman, Cara Fedick, Tyler Frederick, Anne H. Gauthier, Sally Jones, Jiweon Jun, Aaron Lai, Qianhan Lin, Tingting Lu, Fiona Lui, Leslie MacRae, Berenice Monna, José Ignacio Giménez Nadal, Monica Pauls, Cori Pawlak, Andrew Shipley, Cecilia Tinonin, Nuno Torres, Charlemaigne Victorino, and Oiching Yeung. Centre for Time Use Research, University of Oxford, United Kingdom. http://www.

timeuse.org/mtus/U.K. 2000 Time-Use Study; Japan 2001 Time Use Study; Harmonised European Time Use Survey [online database version 2.0]. Created 2005–2007 by Statistics Finland and Statistics Sweden, October 1, 2007. https://www.testh2.scb.se/tus/tus/. Germany 1991 data are from the most recent study we could access. This figure may have changed with the introduction of the Internet and easing of laws that limited store hours since that time. The German time figure is for directional purposes only. The figures do not include travel time to and from the store for the U.S. and Europe. Germany and Japan are undetermined as we could not locate English documentation; however, the low minutes per week relative to other countries suggests that travel is excluded. Statistical analysis and conclusions in this research are those drawn by Exponential Edge Inc. and may not reflect the views of the creators or funders of the harmonized datasets and other data sources. "Internet Activity Index," Online Publishers Association, and Nielsen Online, 2008/2009 online IAI data for the Commerce category for Total Time, Unique Visitors, by month annualized and averaged across 2008/2009, analyzed by Exponential Edge Inc. to derive 37.5 minutes per week per unique visitor (5.36 minutes per day) on average across the period 2008/2009, http://www.online-publishers.org/internet-activity-index (accessed February 2010). This is a good resource for time spent online for the categories of content, commerce, communications, community, and search. Commerce for this purpose is defined as websites and Internet applications that are designed for shopping online but also include sites such as shopping, where payment transactions are measured separately from Yahoo! email services, according to the publisher. Examples of those included in this segment are Amazon, eBay, Shopping.com, and Dell.com. The total minutes spent on commerce across these periods varied from a low of 5.26 minutes per day (May 2009) to a high of 6.65 minutes per day (Jan. 2008). Refer to http://www.online-publishers.org/internet-activity-index for further details on the IAI methodology: Exponential Edge Primary Research conducted July–November 2009. C-Level, VP, Director 10.44% N = 108; Small Business Owners 10.47% of Time Spent Shop/Research/Communicate with vendors for products or services for business N = 90. This survey represents U.S.-based firms. For further details on this research and methodology, please visit our website at www.exponentialedge.com. IDC Special Study, "Sales Enablement 3.0, A Transformation of Sales Enabled by a Transformation of Marketing," IDC #218546, Volume 1, June 2001; IDC Special Study, "An Inconvenient Truth: The Role and Value of Information in the IT Buying Process," IDC#209985, Volume 1, January 2008; Executive Time Spent Will Vary by Function and Lifecycle of a Project. These are averages based on survey responses. Information was also gathered from a direct interview on October 8, 2009, and subsequent email communications with Clare Gillan of International Data Corporation (IDC). To derive the minutes and hours per week we used a 51-hour average work week for executives of large companies. Based on a survey conducted by CIO Magazine as a proxy for complex purchasing processes,"Report: Most Executives Work 50-Hour-Plus Weeks," CIO, April 28, 2006. http://www.cio.com/article/25090/ Report_Most_Executives_Work_50_Hour_Plus_Weeks (accessed October 17, 2009); For U.S. Small Business Owners we used 52 hours per week for average hourly employment from Wells Fargo/Gallup Small Business Index figures, "Small Business Owners Work Long Hours But Manage Work/Life Balance," Accounting Web in CFO, August 30, 2005. http://www.accountingweb.com/ item/101254 (accessed October 17, 2009).

6. A recent study by the Consumer Electronics Institute and Yahoo! found that 77 percent of consumers spent an average of 12 hours online researching electronics before making a purchase. Not surprisingly, the more complex and expensive the offering, the more time spent online. For example, cell phones took an average of nine hours and televisions took 15 hours. Karen M. Cheung, "Majority of Consumers Research Online before Buying," *digitalcamerainfo. com*, October 24, 2006. http://www.digitalcamerainfo.com/content/Majority-of-Consumers-Research-Online-before-Buying.htm.

7. See Introduction, endnote 5.

8. The distribution of time spent purchasing may not be even, and it is expected that there are peaks and valleys; however, this is a calculation of the total time distributed evenly across time. For business buyers, this figure does not include dedicated procurement department personnel that are tasked full time with purchasing commodities such as pencils. This time estimate is most representative of executives purchasing complex lines of business offerings such as IT, and of small business owners who were asked to estimate their time.

9. "Losing Loyalty: The Consumer Defection Dilemma™: A Milestone Study on CPG Brand Loyalty & Defection Among American Shoppers," CMO Council, Pointer Media Network, 2009. http://www.cmocouncil.org/resources/reports/ Losing_Loyalty_023.pdf.

10. Associated Press, "OMG! Italian Catholics Asked to Not Text During Lent," *USA Today*, March 4, 2009.

11. Broadbent and Broadbent, "From Detection to Identification: Response to Multiple Targets in Rapid Serial Visual Presentation," *Perception and Psychophysics* 42 (2), 1987: 105–13.

12. Thomas Koelewijn and Erik Van der Burg, "Attentional Blink and the Stream of Consciousness," *Psyblog*, 2007. www.spring.org.uk/2009/04. Based on auditory studies.

13. Stefanie Olsen, "Digital Kids Grow Up," *CNet News*, December 11, 2007. http:// www.news.com/Year-in-review-Digital-kids-grow-up/2009–1025_3–6222143. html?tag=item.; Financial figures from www.hoovers.com. Ganz is a privately held company. http://www.news.com/Webkinz-I-fell-in-love-with-a-cyber-alley-cat/2100–1026_3–6182834.html?tag=news.1.

14. Laurie Meekis, "Webkinz vs. Beanie Babies 2.0—Can They Catch the Online Wave that Webkinz Started?" *Associated Content*, March 17, 2008. http://www.

associatedcontent.com/article/652605/webkinz_vs_beanie_babies_20_can_
they.html.

15. Nielsen/NetRating, November 2006.

16. www.compete.com (accessed March 2010) for Webkinz.com vs. Ty.com. Com-
pete.com monthly normalized metrics for January 2010 are as follows: Ty.com
(273 thousand) vs. Webkinz.com (4.46 million) U.S. visitors. Webkinz.com has
more than 16 times the visitors of Ty.com.

17. Time-ographics® and Exponential Edge® are registered trademarks filed with
the U.S. Patent and Trademark office. For ease of reading, we will note that it
applies to all uses throughout the book. This does not limit rights in any way.

18. All information in this book is the author's opinion and does not represent that
of clients and affiliates. Data is entirely from publicly available sources, unless
specified as derived from primary research by the author.

19. I use consumer examples extensively because they are easily understood by
many. However, the examples in this book also apply to many business-to-
business situations. Several cases in the book highlight successful business-to-
business situations.

Chapter 1: The Money Value of Time

1. Paul Romer, "Time Is Really Money," *InformationWeek*, September 11, 2000.
The author also had an email exchange with Dr. Romer in late 2009 to confirm
the continued validity of the statement.

2. Mark McClusky, "The Nike Experiment: How the Shoe Giant Unleashed the
Power of Personal Metrics," *Wired Magazine*, June 22, 2009.

3. Sarah Deem, "Nike+ iPod Musical Shoes," *Popular Mechanics*, May 23, 2006;
Steve Jobs, iPod special event recorded on Apple website, September 2007.

4. Reported from the Nike+ statistics website and miles counter, http://nikerun-
ning.nike.com/nikeos/p/nikeplus/en_US/plus/#//dashboard/ (accessed March 10,
2010).

5. Brian Morrissey, "Nike Plus Starts to Open Up to Web," *AdWeek*, July 20, 2009
(accessed August 13, 2009). http://www.adweek.com/aw/content_display/news/
digital/e3ibdf529f18374f6c956632f68978f15bd.

6. Based on the U.S. Labor Department Data for 2008 (released summer 2009) at
27 minutes per day, assuming 16 waking hours per day. Although there are less
data available, our research of international databases indicates about 30 minutes
per day as well in industrialized countries—no significant difference. No data
exists internationally for the amount of time spent over the past four decades.

7. See Introduction, endnote 5, Internet Activity Index.

8. See Introduction, endnote 5, Exponential Edge Primary Research, IDC Special Studies.

9. Trends were derived from the American Heritage Time Use Study (AHTUS)
Historical U.S. Time-Use Data: American Heritage Time Use Study, release 1

(May 2006), created at the Centre for Time Use Research, United Kingdom, by Kimberly Fisher, Muriel Egerton, and Jonathan Gershuny, with Nuno Torres and Andreas Pollmann, and with contributions from Anne H. Gauthier and John Robinson. Created for Yale University with initial funding from the Glaser Progress Foundation and supplementary funding from the ESRC. Statistical analysis and conclusions in this research are those drawn by Exponential Edge Inc. and may not reflect the views of the creators or funders of AHTUS or the collectors of the original surveys harmonized in this dataset: Mark Aguiar and Erik Hurst, "Measuring Trends in Leisure: The Allocation of Time over Five Decades," Working Papers, Federal Reserve Bank of Boston No. 06–02, Version January 2006, Table II. n=27,566 Individuals. For methodology and differences in sampling between this analysis and the ATHUS, see Appendix A of this report of this paper. Note that time in the Aguiar/Hurst analysis includes travel time.

10. Historical U.S. Time-Use Data: American Heritage Time Use Study, release 1 (May 2006), created at the Centre for Time Use Research, United Kingdom, by Kimberly Fisher, Muriel Egerton, and Jonathan Gershuny, with Nuno Torres and Andreas Pollmann, with contributions from Anne H. Gauthier and John Robinson. Created for Yale University with initial funding from the Glaser Progress Foundation and supplementary funding from the ESRC. Statistical analysis and conclusions in this research are those drawn by Exponential Edge Inc. and may not reflect the views of the creators or funders of AHTUS or the collectors of the original surveys harmonized in this dataset.

11. See Introduction, endnote 5. U.S. Trademarks is used as a proxy for the number of products. Although not a perfect measure because not all trademarks are products and some trademarks represent multiple products, it provides a good representation of the growth in product and brand proliferation.

12. Jack Loechner, "8% of Internet Users Account for 85% of All Clicks," *MediaPost-Blogs*, October 13, 2009. http://www.mediapost.com/publications/?fa=Articles. showArticle&art_aid=115210.

13. There are other factors beyond price that impact the equation—intangible benefits, for one. In order to keep this example simple, however, I have not included them. Time has always been an element included in "other," but it is now a major factor in most purchase decisions today and so it is recognized and called out.

14. In a price-elastic market. Of course, in an inelastic market other factors would prevail.

15. It is duly noted that time and attention are not entirely independent variables. There are other variables for time that would be more accurate from a theoretical standpoint but would serve to confuse the reader and would not result in a better action or outcome. I am opting for simplicity that drives success and comprehension over theoretical accuracy and complexity. The differences between the actions and product attributes for each of the quadrants are distinct,

as will be shared throughout this book. The "propensity for time" is actually a combination of the "propensity to spend time," where a person willingly spends time as evidenced in the motivation quadrant, and tasks that have a tendency to consume time repeatedly, such as habits and background business processes. I am using the term "propensity for time" to represent both of these conditions. The same holds true for "propensity for attention," where there is a propensity to devote attention, as in the motivation quadrant, and a tendency to utilize attention, as in the convenience quadrant when we are in urgent need of a service. "Propensity for attention" covers both of these conditions.

16. Tom, "Fat habits," Duke Research Blog, Duke University, February 28, 2008. http://dukeresearch.blogspot.com/2008_02_03_archive.html (accessed July 2009); Mindy Ji Song and Wendy Wood, "Habitual Purchase and Consumption Habits: Not Always What You Intend," *Journal of Consumer Psychology* 17(4), 2007: 261–76; Wendy Wood, Jeffrey M. Quinn, and Deborah A. Kashy, "Habits in Everyday Life: Thought, Emotion, and Action," *Journal of Personality and Social Psychology* 83 (6), 2002: 1281–97.

17. J Sainsbury PLC, "Annual Report and Financial Statements 2009," May 2009. http://www.j-sainsbury.co.uk/ar09/flash/alternative/sleepshopping.shtml (accessed October 18, 2009). For ease of reading, we will note that it applies to all uses throughout the book. This does not limit rights in any way.

18. Mihály Csíkszentmihályi, *Flow*, Harper Perennial, 1991.

19. Calculated as follows: 126Bits/second divided by 7 bits per letter = number of letters per second. Number of letters per second divided by 4.5 letters per average word in English = 4 words per second ([40 bps (listening)]/126 maximum) multiplied by 4 words per second = 1.27 words per second. 4.5average letters per word used from Trinity College Website Computer Science Department Website, http://starbase.trincoll.edu/~crypto/resources/LetFreq.html (accessed October 3, 2009).

20. This assumes human information is absorbed at maximum 126bps capacity for 16 waking hours per day. Internet transfer is at 2 MBPS, resulting in approximately 29 hours to transfer.

21. Visual Cognition Lab, University of Illinois. http://viscog.beckman.illinois.edu/djs_lab/demos.html. This page contains a number of interesting videos that document this effect. The results are for two people that were not in the same social group, e.g., one much older than the other. Results were higher for students (in-group) but dipped to 35 percent noticing when one of the students was dressed as a construction worker.

22. Natalie Angier, "Brain is a Co-Conspirator in a Vicious Stress Loop," *New York Times*, August 18, 2009.

23. Retrieved on December 31, 2007. "Exposure to moderately bright light (~450 lux; ~1.2 W/m2) for the second or first half of the scheduled wake episode is effective for entraining individuals to the 24.65-h Martian sol and a 23.5-h day length, respectively." Via Wikipedia under "Free-Running Sleep."

24. John Travis, "Biological Stopwatch Found in the Brain," *Science News*, February 17, 1996. http://www.sciencenews.org/pages/pdfs/data/1996/149–07/14907–09.pdf (accessed August 15, 2009).

25. Sandra Blakeslee, "Running Late, Researchers Blame Aging Again," *New York Times*, March 24, 1998.

26. "The Science of Addiction Simplified," Center of Substance Abuse Treatment, U.S. Department of Health and Human Services, July 1999. http://pbrownacsw.com/scienceofaddictionsimplified.htm (accessed August 15, 2009).

27. Ibid., 26.

28. Ibid., 26.

29. Emily Yoffie, "Seeking: Why the Brain Hard-Wires Us to Like Google, Twitter and Texting, and Why That's Dangerous," *Slate*, August 12, 2009. http://www.slate.com/id/2224932/pagenum/all/#p2. Other theories as to evoking desire called "wanting" by Ken Barridge exist that affect different bodily functions. The differences extend beyond the scope of this discussion, which is pertaining to desire versus reward, which is consistent in research.

30. Bob Holmes, "Why Time Flies in Old Age," *New Scientist*, Issue 2057, November 23, 1996.

31. R. J. Rummel, *Understanding Conflict and War, Vol. 1: The Dynamic Psychological Field* (Beverly Hills: Sage Publications, 1975), Chapter 15: *Situation, Expectations, and Triggers accessed January 6, 2010 at http://www.hawaii.edu/powerkills/DPF.CHAP15.HTM.*

32. "Appendix—Additional Findings and Presentation Materials," Center for Research Excellence, June 8, 2009 via http://www.researchexcellence.com/vc-mstudy.php. The CRE is an independent group funded by Nielsen. The study was conducted by Ball State University Center for Media Design.

33. Alison Bond, "Key Brain Section Never Multitasks—It Just Switches Very Fast," *Discover Blogs, Mind & Brain*, July 20, 2009. http://blogs.discovermagazine.com/80beats/2009/07/20/key-brain-section-never-multitasks%E2%80%94it-just-switches-very-fast/.

34. Claudia Wallis, "Are Kids Too Wired for Their Own Good?" *Time Magazine*, March 27, 2006.

35. Christine Rosen, "The Myth of Multitasking," *The New Atlantis*, Number 20, Spring 2008: 105–10.

36. Clifford Nass, interview by NPR Science Friday, "Multitasking May Not Mean Higher Productivity," August 26, 2009. The question about real-world multitasking by women was answered by Mr. Nass during the interview during approximately minutes 10:40 and 11:40, where he suggested a large body of literature that supported this. The biological origin is my opinion and was not stated by Mr. Nass.

37. Ibid., 34.

38. Michelle Conlin, "Take a Vacation from Your BlackBerry," *BusinessWeek*, December 20, 2004. http://www.businessweek.com/magazine/content/04_51/b3913089.htm (accessed October 18, 2009).

39. Marisa Taylor, "Why Multitaskers Stink at Multitasking," *WSJ Blogs*, August 26, 2009. http://blogs.wsj.com/digits/2009/08/26/why-multitaskers-stink-at-multi-tasking/; Adam Gorlick, "Media Multitaskers Pay Mental Price, Stanford Study Shows," *Stanford Report*, August 24, 2009. http://news.stanford.edu/news/2009/august24/multitask-research-study–082409.html; Clifford Nass, interview by NPR Science Friday.

40. Ibid., 34.

41. "Online Opens Multi-Media Doors for Marketers," *Online Sights by Burst Media*, October 2007. http://burstmedia.com/pdfs/research/2007_10_01.pdf.

42. Certainly, the customer considers other factors in a purchase decision; convenience is a good example. However, the center of gravity resides in the value quadrant, with other considerations as secondary. For example, most customers shop at Walmart for value, even though it may have attributes of convenience. The center of gravity concept applies to the other quadrants as well.

Chapter 2: Customer Time-Value Innovation Tools and Strategies

1. From interviews in person and via email with the author in mid-2009 to March 2010.

2. Trip Hawkins provided this information during our interview and in subsequent emails in 2009 and in March 2010.

3. "The Way the Brain Buys," *Economist*, December 18, 2008. www.economist.com/science/displaystory.com?story_id=12792420.

4. Kate Stein, "Shop Faster," *New York Times*, April 15, 2009.

5. "The Way the Brain Buys," *Economist*, December 18, 2008. www.economist.com/science/displaystory.com?story_id=12792420.

6. The concept "Awareness, Consideration, Preference, Consideration, Purchase, Delivery" has existed in marketing practice for many years and there are variations of this purchasing funnel in existence. The source is unknown even though it is commonly used in marketing.

7. Deborah Yao, "More Ads Coming to TV—Even to One-Time Havens," Associated Press, August 2, 2009.

8. Full disclosure: the author and her firm, Exponential Edge Inc., have provided consulting services to ZillionTV.

9. Ibid., 7.

10. Ibid., 7.

11. "Increase Sales with Color, Sound, Taste, Smell, and Touch," *Marketing Profs Tutorial*, March 8, 2001. http://www.marketingprofs.com (accessed July 24, 2009).

12. Adrian C. North, David J. Hargreaves, and Jennifer McKendrick, "In-Store Music Affects Product Choice," *Nature* 390, 1997: 132; Adrian C. North, David J. Hargreaves, and Jennifer McKendrick, "The Influence of In-Store Music on Wine Selections," *Journal of Applied Psychology* 84, 1999: 271–76; Tania Gabrielle French,"How Music Affects Your Buying Habits." April 27, 2006. http://www.pickbrains.com (accessed August 5, 2009).

13. J. Hornick, "Tactile Stimulation and Consumer Response," *Journal of Consumer Research* Vol. 19, No. 3 (Dec. 1992): 449–58.

14. Sandra Blakeslee, "Running Late, Researchers Blame Aging Again," *New York Times*, March 24, 1998.

15. Roger Dooley, "Does Your Marketing Smell?" *FutureLab*, July 31, 2007. This article referenced an experiment cited by Martin Lindstromm, author of *Brandsense*, conducted on Nike Shoes.

16. Karen Ravn, "Sniff . . . and Spend—Scents such as Lilac, Chocolate and Vanilla Can Seduce Us to Part with Our Cash. Ready Your Nose for the Mall," *Los Angeles Times*, August 20, 2007.

17. About Us Section, www.dailylit.com.

18. Marissa Miley, "DailyLit Rolling Out a Novel Idea for Ads," *AdvertisingAge.com* on *CrainsNewYorkBusiness.com*. http://www.crainsnewyork.com/apps/pbcs.dll/article?AID=/20081224/FREE/812249995/1040.

19. Elizabeth Chuck, "Leasing luxury: Designer handbags for rent," MSNBC.com, October 31, 2006. http://www.msnbc.msn.com/id/14294163/ (accessed March 11, 2010).

20. Jamie LaReau, "GM to Dealers: OnStar Can Be a Tool to Boost Service Revenue," *Automotive News*, May 4, 2009, via Encyclopedia Britannica online accessed November 23, 2009. http://www.britannica.com/bps/additional-content/18/41779261/GM-to-dealers-OnStar-can-be-tool-to-boost-service-revenue.

21. Stuart Dredge, "Digital Chocolate Unveils Nanostars Virtual Items Platform," *Mobile Entertainment News*, September 23, 2009. http://www.mobile-ent.biz/news/34460/Digital-Chocolate-unveils-NanoStars-virtual-items-platform.

22. See Introduction, endnote 5, "Internet Activity Index."

23. Judy Motti, "Is Amazon Prepping a Kindle Redux?" *Internet.com*, January 28, 2009. www.internetnews.com/ec-news/print.php/3799226.

24. Chris Anderson, *Free: The Future of a Radical Price* (New York: Hyperion, 2009).

25. Ismat Sarah Mangla, "If They Built the Perfect Bank," *Money Magazine*, December 2009, information contained in the sidebar "Ready to Switch?," p. 93.

Chapter 3: Time Magnets: Motivation Quadrant Products

1. IDC Special Study, "An Inconvenient Truth: The Role and Value of Information in the IT Buying Process," IDC#209985, Volume 1, January 2008. The time represented is from pre-crash 2008 findings, when buying was more normalized and expected to be less restricted than with the economic downturn. The level of time is expected to peak just prior to a large decision; this is an average that is spread across an entire workday.

2. Dr. Mihály Csíkszentmihályi, as quoted in "Flow (psychology)," *Wikipedia*. http://en.wikipedia.org/wiki/Flow_(psychology).

3. www.geocache.com. Approximate number of geocaches in New York metro area based on Googlemaps rendering as of March 7, 2010.

4. I am told that several Starbucks locations on the East Coast of the United States have replaced their chairs with hard chairs, making them less comfortable.

5. Douglas MacMillan, "Facebook Banks on a Little Help from Its Friends," *BusinessWeek*, October 15, 2009.

6. To view these entertaining VW videos, go to http://www.thefuntheory.com.

7. *PRWeek*, "Cause Survey 2007," PrWeek/Barkley Public Relations, October 22, 2007. Consumer Support Question n = 225.

8. Press release, *Cone Cause Evolution Survey of American Buyers*, 2008. www.coneinc.com/content1188.; *PRWeek*, "Cause Survey 2007."

9. A widget is a downloadable micro-application that streams updates to a desktop, mobile device, or Web page on an ongoing basis. Widgets are often used to track moving data points such as ongoing stock quotes or weather.

10. The Pampers widget can be found at http://www.pampers.com/en_US/PregnancyWidget.

11. Pampers Village can be found at http://www.pampers.com/en_US/home.

12. Julia Angwin and Emily Steel, "Founders Step Aside at MySpace," *Wall Street Journal*, April 25, 2009.

13. Gary Rivlin, "Wallflower at the Web Party," *New York Times*, October 15, 2006.

14. www.wamu.com.

15. Robin Sidel, "FDIC and WaMu's Branches Lose the Smiles," *Wall Street Journal*, April 7, 2009.

16. Dave, "iPhone 3G Overtakes RAZR as Top U.S. Consumer Handset," *MacBlogz*, November 10, 2008. Based on numbers from NPD Group. Also based on introduction dates from Wikipedia.

Chapter 4: Time on Autopilot: Habit Quadrant Products

1. Tom, "Fat Habits," *Duke Research Blog*, February 28, 2008. http://dukeresearch.blogspot.com/2008_02_03_archive.html (accessed November 2009).

2. The quote is based on an email conversation with Dr. Sigman dated November 29, 2009, based on his quotes in the following article: Ruki Sayid, "Your Life: Talking Shop," *RedOrbitNews*, November 3, 2005. http://www.redorbit.com/news/science/293768/your_life_talking_shop__sleep_shopping/ (accessed October 31, 2009).

3. Site Rankings for Daily Time Spent on Site for Google.com over three months, average 11.32 minutes per day, http://www.alexa.com/siteinfo/google.com (accessed March 10, 2010).

4. comScore Press Release, comScore Releases February 2010, U.S. Search Engine Rankings, Reston, VA March 10, 2010, http://www.comscore.com/Press_Events/Press_Releases/2010/3/comScore_Releases_February_2010_U.S._Search_Engine_Rankings (accessed March 11, 2010).

5. Henry Blodget, "Google Solid Q1, Amazing Cash Flow," *The Business Insider*, April 16, 2009.

6. Author's Note: Information about Microsoft is entirely from publicly available sources. All information in this book is the author's opinion and does not represent that of clients and affiliates.

7. Jessica Hodson, "Microsoft's Ad Campaign to take on Google's Dominance," *Wall Street Journal*, June 3, 2009.

8. John Paczkowski, "Microsoft CEO Steve Ballmer: Bing!" *D7 Highlights*, May 28 2009. http://d7.allthingsd.com/20090528/d7-interview-steve-ballmer/.

9. Nicholas Carson, "Ballmer Says He'll Spend as Much as $11 Billion on Search," *The Business Insider*, June 18, 2009. http://www.businessinsider.com/ballmer-says-hell-spend–11-billion-on-search–2009–6.

10. News release, "Bing Search Increases 22 Percent Month-Over-Month in August, According to Nielsen," September 14, 2009. http://en-us.nielsen.com/main/news/news_releases/2009/september/bing_search_increases (accessed October 30, 2009).

11. Mark Buchanan, "Why We Are All Creatures of Habit," *NewScientist*, July 4, 2007.

12. Ibid., 11.

13. Professor Sandy Pentland as quoted in Ibid., 11.

14. Natalie Angier, "Brain is a Co-Conspirator in a Vicious Stress Loop," *New York Times*, August 18, 2009. This research was conducted on rats and suggests that the same applies to humans, although it is not proven.

15. This is one of the key differences between this quadrant and the convenience quadrant, where the most salient goal is saving time. Time has two elements in this context. Often in the habit quadrant our desire is to *outsource* time. Telephones don't process calls more quickly and banks don't run transactions more quickly as a result of buying these services. We "save time" because we've outsourced it to another service in the background and don't need to pay attention to it. This differs from certain products in the convenience quadrant that actually compress the amount of time something takes to complete, such as overnight package delivery or faster lunch ordering. Both elements, outsourcing and compressing, can ultimately reside in the habit quadrant. Neuroscientists have found that habits become grooved into the limbic system in the brain. With system background processes, the brain is not affected in the same way.

16. B. J. Fogg, "A Behavior Model for Persuasive Design," *Persuasive '09*, paper, 2009 ACM ISBN 978–1–60558–376–1/09/04. http://www.bjfogg.com/fbm_files/page4_1.pdf (accessed January 9, 2010).

17. Sarah Mahoney, "Average CMO Tenure Creeps over the Two-Year Mark," *Marketing Daily*, June 13, 2007. http://www.mediapost.com/publications/index.cfm?fa=Articles.showArticle&art_aid=62277 (accessed November 1, 2009). The article cites a study conducted by Spencer Stuart that tracked CMOs at 100 leading consumer companies at 26.8 months.

18. Emmett C. Murphy and Mark A. Murphy, *Leading on the Edge of Chaos* (Paramus, N.J.: Prentice-Hall Press, 2002).

19. B. Wanskick, J. E. Painter, and Y. K. Lee, "The Office Candy Dish: Proximity's Influence and Actual Consumption," *International Journal of Obesity (Lond)* 30(5), 2006: 871–75.

20. T. A. Farley and D. A. Cohen, "Eating as an Automatic Behavior," *Preventing Chronic Disease* 5(1), 2008. http://www.cdc.gov/pcd/issues/2008/jan/07_0046. htm (accessed July 24, 2009).

21. B. J. Fogg, *Persuasive Technology* (San Francisco: Morgan Kauffman, 2003), pp. 103–4.

22. http://www.vivecoach.com (accessed October 31, 2009). Based on reviews, telephone interviews, and email exchanges with founders Doug Keare and Jennifer Gill Roberts beginning in October 2009.

23. Not all products or services are suited to the habit quadrant—there are products that are high frequency, provide fast feedback, and are ongoing in use but can't become brain habits. For example, most of us drive our cars every day, and if they are in good working order, they provide, quite literally, fast feedback. But the habit of driving a car is never going to become a habit that benefits the automaker. Why? Because the purchase price of a car is so high that a driver's mental alarm goes off and turns off the autopilot.

24. Jeremy Dean, "How Long to Form a Habit?" *Psyblog*, date unknown. http://www.spring.org.uk/2009/09/how-long-to-form-a-habit.php (accessed October 31, 2009).

25. Philippa Lally, Cornelia H. H. Van Jaarsveld, Henry W. W. Potts, and Jane Wardle, "How Are Habits Formed: Modelling Habit Formation in the Real World," *European Journal of Social Psychology*, 2009, cited in Wikipedia, Lally P, van Jaarsveld CHM, Potts H, Wardle J (2009). "How are habits formed: Modelling habit formation in the real world." *European Journal of Social Psychology*, Early View. DOI: 10.1002/ejsp.674.

26. The Associated Press, "U.S. businesses hype hand sanitizers," CBC News, January 4, 2007. http://www.cbc.ca/news/story/2007/01/04/hand-sanitizer.html (accessed March 11, 2010).

27. Interview with Carol Berning, consumer psychologist, retired, P&G, November 6, 2009 and subsequent communications.

28. Charles Duhigg, "Warning: Habits May Be Good for You," *New York Times*, July 13, 2008.

29. P&G press release, "Ten Years Marks Milestone for Proctor & Gamble's Febreze Brand," June 4, 2009. http://www.pginvestor.com/phoenix.zhtml?c=104574&p=irol-newsArticle&ID=1162213&highlight= (accessed November 1, 2009).

30. International Telecommunications Union Report (ITU), a UN Organization, 2008.

31. Walt Albro, "A Switch in Time: You Can Attract Big Deposits by Making It Convenient for Prospects to Transfer Their Accounts to Your Financial Institution," *ABA Bank Marketing*, July 1, 2005. http://www.accessmylibrary.com/ar

ticle–1G1–135000593/switch-time-you-can.html (accessed November 1, 2009). Banks today are using a variety of approaches to accomplish this goal.

32. Jennifer Davies and Keith Darce, "Last Grocery Strike's Effect Still Felt," *Union-Tribune*, March 4, 2007.

33. "Whole Foods Benefits from Calif. Grocery Strike," *Austin Business Journal*, February 27, 2004.

34. Davies and Darce, "Last Grocery Strike's Effect Still Felt," *Union-Tribune*, March 4, 2007. Andrew Wolf, who covers the grocery industry for BB&T Capital Markets, indicated that the market shares are not back to what they once were.

35. Ibid., 34.

36. Karen Blumenthal, "In the Fight Against Bill Creep, Every Extra Fee Is the Enemy," *Wall Street Journal*, January 28, 2009.

Chapter 5: Time Savers: Convenience Quadrant Products

1. Interview with ZoomSystems CEO Gower Smith on November 23, 2009; ZoomSystems press release, "Zoom Systems Recognized for Excellence Across Multiple Channels," March 24, 2009.

2. If you have a vertically integrated product, it might be necessary to break it apart in order to conduct a proper Time-ographics analysis. It depends on the context.

3. Consumer Federation of America press release, "New Report Shows Consumers Underestimate the Value of Comparison Shopping," April 16, 2003.

4. Exponential Edge Primary Research, 2008.

5. Farhad Jamjoo, "That Tune, Named, How Does the Music-Identifying App Shazam Work Its Magic?" *Slate*, October 19, 2009. http://www.slate.com/id/2232914/ (accessed October 20, 2009).

6. Intuit Small Business website. http://www.intuit.com/ (accessed November 17, 2009).

7. Some perishable items will not transition to the habit quadrant because they are less frequent and regular. In this case the replenishment for most customers is not frequent enough to transition into the habit quadrant. Other products that are more perishable and need frequent replenishment would qualify for transition to this habit quadrant. The resulting actions and market traction benefits do not change for these products.

8. From a primary interview with Doug Greenberg, vice president of marketing and sales, Garde Robe, on November 11, 2009, and from subsequent communications with him and his team; information was also collected from the Garde Robe website http://www.garderobeonline.com/garderobepage/sortingpage.html (accessed December 2009 and March 8, 2010).

9. David Leonhardt, "Comparison of FreshDirect Prices to Other Stores," *New York Times*, November 21, 2006. http://www.nytimes.com/2006/11/21/

business/22leonhardt-side.html?_r=1&ex=1174104000&en=446bfd0c08fb5281
&ei=5070 (accessed October 1, 2009).

10. Virginia Heffernan, "Produce Yourself," *New York Times*, October 12, 2008.
http://www.nytimes.com/2008/10/12/magazine/12wwln-medium-t.html?
pagewanted=print; accessed August 12, 2009. This article provides background
and user context for this case.

Chapter 6: Time Minimized: Value Quadrant Products

1. See Chapter 1, note 42.
2. Kenneth Davids with Ted Stachura, "McDonald's vs. Starbucks: A Milky Skir-
mish in the Coffee Wars," *The Coffee Review*, May 2009. http://www.coffeere-
view.com/article.cfm?ID=158 (accessed March 10, 2010).
3. Jen Abelson, "Coffee Competition," *Boston Globe*, June 18, 2009. http://www.
boston.com/business/articles/2009/06/18/mcdonalds_gains_ground_on_cof-
fee_rivals_dunkin_starbucks/ (accessed March 11, 2010); BIGResearch Press
Release, "Coffee Wars, Starbucks Still #1, McDonald's #2, and Rising, Dunkin'
Donuts #3," Market Wire 5/28/09.
4. Nancy Trejos, "Recession Lesson: Share and Swap Replaces Grab and Buy,"
Washington Post, July 17, 2009. http://www.washingtonpost.com/wp-dyn/con-
tent/article/2009/07/16/AR2009071604201_2.html?sid=ST2009071604213 (accessed March 10, 2010).
5. From the Zipcar website, http://www.zipcar.com/how (accessed March 10, 2010).
6. James K. Binley and John Bejnarowicz, "Consumer Price Awareness in Food
Shopping: The Case of Quantity Surcharges," *Journal of Retailing* 79(1), 2003:
27–35; Enrique Manzur and Sergio Olavarrieta, "Retailers Price Promotion
Strategies and Its Effect on Consumers' Price Perceptions and Search Behavior," paper presented at the BALAS Annual Conference, Universidad de los
Andes School of Management, Bogota, D.C., Colombia, April 23, 2008, http://
www.allacademic.com/meta/p233054_index.html.
7. Available at this price in the United States on October 28, 2009 from http://www.
walmart.com/search/search-ng.do?search_constraint=0&ic=48_0&search_
query=caskets&Find.x=0&Find.y=0&Find=Find.
8. James Surowiecki, "Priced to Go," *The New Yorker*, November 9, 2009.
9. *SC Digest* editorial staff, "Procurement Benchmarks Show Wide Variation between Top and Bottom Performers," *Supply Chain Digest*, October 4, 2006. http://
www.scdigest.com/assets/newsviews/06–10–04–2.cfm?cid=774&ctype=content.
10. "Serial Position Effect," *Wikipedia*. http://en.wikipedia.org/wiki/Serial_posi-
tion_effect (accessed October 28, 2009); P. A. Frensch, "Composition during
Serial Learning: A Serial Position Effect," *Journal of Experimental Psychology*:
Learning, Memory, and Cognition 20 (2), 1994: 423–43; A. F. Healy, D. A. Ha-
vas, and J. T. Parkour, "Comparing Serial Position Effects in Semantic and
Episodic Memory Using Reconstruction of Order Tasks," *Journal of Memory*

and Language 42, 2000: 147–67; Murray Glanzer and Anita R. Cunitz, "Two Storage Mechanisms in Free Recall," *Journal of Verbal Learning and Verbal Behaviour* 5 (1966): 351–60; James Deese and Robert A. Kaufman, "Serial Effects in Recall of Unorganized and Sequentially Organized Verbal Material," *Journal of Experimental Psychology* 54(3), 1957: 180–87; B. B. Murdock Jr., "The Serial Position Effect of Free Recall," *Journal of Experimental Psychology* 64 (1962): 482–88; M. Glanzer and A. R. Cunitz, "Two Storage Mechanisms in Free Recall," *Journal of Verbal Learning and Verbal Behaviour* 5 (1966): 351–60; Christine Kohler, "Order Effects Theory: Primacy versus Recency," Center for Interactive Advertising, The University of Texas at Austin. http://www.ciadvertising.org/sa/spring_04/adv382j/christine/primacy.html (accessed November 04, 2009); Yvonne de Kort, Wijnand IJsselsteijn, Cees J. H. Midden, Berry Eggen, and B. J. Fogg, eds., *Persuasive Technology, Second International Conference on Persuasive Technology*, PERSUASIVE 2007. Palo Alto, CA, USA, April 26-27, 2007. Revised Selected Papers. Lecture Notes in Computer Science 4744, Springer 2007.

11.   de Kort et al., Ibid.

12.   Ibid., 11.

13.   Mirela Iverac, "The Upside of Bad Online Customer Reviews." *Forbes.com*, August 4, 2009. http://www.forbes.com/2009/08/04/bad-customer-reviews-entrepreneurs-management-ebags.html (accessed October 27, 2009).

14.   David Gianatasio, "Nielsen: Consumers Trust Online Opinions," *AdWeek*, July 7, 2009. http://www.intuit.com/http://www.adweek.com/aw/content_display/news/agency/e3i0a5fa05df2f2bdcfe08f71da7df1e37a?pn=1 (accessed October 24, 2009).

Chapter 7: Innovating Customer Time-Value into Market Traction

1.   "Global Strategy on Diet, Physical Activity and Health—Diabetes," World Health Organization. http://www.who.int/dietphysicalactivity/publications/facts/diabetes/en/index.html (accessed September 12, 2009). This population represents 23.6 million people, with 17.9 million diagnosed and 5.7 million undiagnosed people. Costs to the United States are $174 billion in direct ($116 billion medical costs) and $58 billion in indirect (e.g., disability, work loss, premature mortality) costs to the U.S. economy.

2.   "National Diabetes Fact Sheet," U.S. Centers for Disease Control (CDC), 2007. http://www.cdc.gov/diabetes/pubs/pdf/ndfs_2007.pdf (accessed September 27, 2009).

3.   Information on the Johnson & Johnson case study is based on a primary interview with Eric Compton and Stephanie Wenstrup on August 4, 2009. Further information was garnered from subsequent communication with Eric Compton. Some of the background information on the inTouch™ diabetes offering was pulled from the Johnson & Johnson website. http://www.symcare.com/ (accessed September 14, 2009).

4. "Global Strategy on Diet, Physical Activity and Health—Diabetes," World Health Organization. http://www.who.int/dietphysicalactivity/publications/facts/diabetes/en/index.html (accessed September 12, 2009).

5. Although starting with the customer is theoretically ideal, the main purpose of the first exercise is to gain a grounding as to where you stand. Unless we are conducting a "blue sky" analysis where no market or no product business exists today, what I have learned through practical experience is that if we begin with the second exercise, namely the customer analysis, sometimes it is easy to over-analyze and "boil the ocean" because customer activities that surface with this approach are often unrelated to your current business competencies. Of course if there is no product, then starting with the customer is logical.

6. The viewpoints on this example are my own directional analysis and not neces-sarily that of Johnson & Johnson. It is recognized that there are many complexi-ties and nuances to diabetic patient activity and the glucose meter market that would factor into this analysis; however, these factors are not useful for demon-strating the general process outlined in this chapter.

7. Wendy Wood and David T. Neal, "A New Look at Habits and the Habit-Goal Interface," *Psychological Review* 114, no. 4 (2007): 843–63.

8. Interview with Carol Berning on November 6, 2009.

9. "Show Me the Money: Quicken 2006 Provides Instant Insights into Spend-ing Habits," *Intuit*, August 1, 2005. http://web.intuit.com/about_intuit/press_releases/2005/08–01a.html (accessed October 10, 2009).

10. This is based on my interview with Mark Nelsen and Margarita Quihuis of Stanford's Persuasive Technology Lab on October 2, 2009, and subsequent emails.

11. B. J. Fogg, *Persuasive Technology: Using Computers to Change What We Think and Do* (San Francisco: Morgan Kaufmann Publishers, 2003).

Chapter 8: The Future of the 24-Hour Customer

1. *Bell Laboratories RECORD* 47(5), May/June 1969: 134–53 and 160–87, a col-lection of several articles on the AT&T Picturephone (then about to be re-leased). http://www.porticus.org/bell/pdf/picturephone.pdf.

2. For a survey on HP challenges during the 1990s, see Sandra Hirsh, Abigail Sellen, and Nancy Brokopp, "Why HP People Do and Don't Use Videoconfer-encing Systems," HP Laboratories, Palo Alto, HPL–2004–140(R.1), February 4, 2005. http://www.hpl.hp.com/techreports/2004/HPL–2004–140R1.pdf (ac-cessed November 7, 2009).

3. The information on Cisco TelePresence was gathered in primary interviews and emails with Brad Whitworth of Cisco during October and November 2009.

4. Bill Gates, "A Robot in Every Home," *ScientificAmerican.com*, January 2007. http://www.scientificamerican.com/article.cfm?id=a-robot-in-every-home (ac-cessed November 8, 2009).

5. P. W. Singer, "Attack of the Military Drones," *Brookings*, June 27, 2009. http://
    www.brookings.edu/opinions/2009/0627_drones_singer.aspx (accessed No-
    vember 7, 2009).

6. P. W. Singer, *Wired for War: The Robotics Revolution and Conflict in the 21st
    Century* (New York: The Penguin Press, 2009).

7. Nic Robertson, "Remote Warfare Ushers A New Kind of Stress," *CNN.com*,
    July 24, 2009. http://edition.cnn.com/2009/WORLD/americas/07/23/wus.war-
    fare.pilots.uav/index.html.

8. Clive Thompson, "Meet the Life Hackers," *New York Times*, October 16, 2005.
    This information from Microsoft is based entirely upon public information
    sources.

INDEX